FATHERS
MATTER

To my friend Topaz!

Thank you for your support.!

Kevin Scotty Greenwood

10/2/21

FATHERS MATTER

VOICES, INSIGHT, AND
REFLECTIONS FROM BLACK
MEN ON POSITIVE PARENTING

ANTHONY & TYREESE R. MCALLISTER

publish
y*our* gift

FATHERS MATTER

Copyright © 2021 Anthony McAllister

Published by Publish Your Gift®
An imprint of Purposely Created Publishing Group, LLC

Printed in the United States of America

ISBN: 978-1-64484-377-2 (print)
ISBN: 978-1-64484-378-9 (ebook)

Special discounts are available on bulk quantity purchases by book clubs, associations and special interest groups. For details email: sales@publishyourgift.com or call (888) 949-6228.
For information logon to: www.PublishYourGift.com

This book grants a glimpse into the complexity of fatherhood in the Black context. A work that highlights the importance of fatherhood and its power to influence the next generation is critical. May these pages reinforce the need for substantive relationships that mold and shape our future leaders. Congratulations to those who shared their stories that inspire and challenge others to make a difference.

"Listen to advice and accept discipline, and at the end you will be counted among the wise." — Proverbs 19:20, NIV

Dr. Lloyd T. McGriff
Senior Pastor, Galilee Baptist Church

TABLE OF CONTENTS

ACKNOWLEDGMENTS

We honor God, "The Father," who birthed the vision for *Fathers Matter* and the fruit it will bear.

Dr. Lloyd T. McGriff, **Senior Pastor, Galilee Baptist Church**, thank you for your spiritual leadership and for Galilee Baptist Church's followship and fellowship.

Deepest appreciation to Dr. Andrew A. Ray, 39th Grand Basileus, Omega Psi Phi Fraternity, Inc., whose servanthood position and foreword offer credibility and encouragement to *Fathers Matter* and the fatherhood journey.

Deep gratitude to the coauthors who have laid their souls on the altar for God's glory and our good.

We are grateful for the assistance of Rev. Lillie I. Sanders and Ms. Ana T. Bolden for their dedicated editing services.

Deepest appreciation to family and friends for prayers and support.

FOREWORD

As the 39th Grand Basileus of Omega Psi Phi Fraternity, Inc., it gives me great pleasure to lend my support to this most timely and important project. Brother Anthony J. McAllister, a thirty-three-year member of Omega Psi Phi Fraternity, Inc., suffered the unthinkable in March 2017 as his 18-year-old daughter, Ayana, was killed by a stray bullet while home on spring break in her freshman year at Saint Augustine's University. This tragic event could have left him broken, but he leaned on God and the cardinal principle of perseverance, and he and his wife triumphed over their tragedy and continue to serve their community in the fight against gun violence. This anthology will give the reader insight into fathers sharing their plight of being fathers, whether they are single dads, stepdads, men who desire to tell their stories of how they had fathers who played phenomenal roles in their lives, men who had fathers who were not a part of their lives as they grew up but made amends in adulthood, or men who simply had absent fathers throughout their lives. Whatever lies in the heart of fathers, this anthology will give the reader an up-close-and-personal glimpse into the lives of fathers telling their stories of how they let go and let God.

Male vs. Manhood

Historically and in current society, the Black male is readily seen, but not the Black Man. Often, there is a tendency to see the Black male and the Black man as one and the same. I urge all to consider the dichotomy between male and man. Being a male is nature's decision. Being a man speaks to one's character as he journeys through life. Therefore, one can be born male and grow into manhood. Conversely, one can be born male and remain so.

I was born and grew up in the segregated South, where one could possibly exist as a male, and dangerously so as a Black man. Working for poverty pay and staying in one's place was a recognized condition for a Black male. There was often a negative view of a Black male who sought to improve his educational and economic conditions, which were expressions of Black manhood.

In my youth, I had the good fortune to be mentored by my parents, pastors, teachers, and community members, who did so via example. They started as agricultural workers and housekeepers in Mississippi. I, too, was a worker. They soon moved to New Orleans to improve our family condition. I remained with my grandparents and started elementary school in a two-room church structure. We were not permitted to attend the town school (for whites only).

My parents were soon able to bring my siblings and me to live in New Orleans. Before leaving Mississippi, my grandmother gave me advice that has endured. She said, "Baby, as you grow up, learn to hold your peace." She advised to always "think before you act." This advice saved my life several years later at the Mardi Gras. There were sections of the city defined by named streets in which Black youth could not safely travel. On seeing the street sign, I stopped. My friend continued for a few yards, where a white officer hit him and knocked him out cold. The officer pulled his gun, put it to my head, spit in my face, and yelled, "You want to hit me, don't you boy? Go on, hit me." I responded, "No, sir, I do not want to hit you." He stared at me for a few seconds, put his gun back in his holster, and said, "Pick up that piece of trash (my friend) and both of you get the hell out of here."

I often share my experience when speaking with youth who are in detention. At one event, a youth responded, "Dr. Ray, you let him punk you like that. He wouldn't have done that to me." I calmly replied, "That's why I am here to tell you about it. I did not respond like you just did. I held my peace." The young man mused, "You had a piece (a gun) and didn't do nothing." This exchange amplified the need for Black men to improve the mentorship of our youth. It exposes one of the disconnects in the transference of survivability to our youth. Across this nation, especially with Black males, "how to get to tomorrow" has been lost.

In my vast arena of life experiences, I have found that both adults and youth have tended to move into silos via the labels of the day, namely old school vs. new school. The continuous drift into silos has interrupted the transference of survivability. I have found that applicable metaphors may have served to bring life-changing clarity to the many conditions along one's life journey. Generationally, life can be viewed as a relay race. Each of us gets a leg of the race to run. It is my hope that we will run our leg of the race to the best of our ability, for our lane will run out, and we must hand off. If the handoff is missed, not only do you lose individually, the whole team loses. Too often, the Black man has missed the handoff to the Black male. The results of the missed handoffs can be seen in parents burying their children, high dropout and failure in educational arenas, reduced economic opportunities, and a perpetual three-sixty of negative outcomes.

Black Men who have succeeded must share the lessons learned with those who are to follow or must run the next leg of the race. This must entail Black men not allowing the change in their respective zip codes to change their moral code. One's zip code gives a physical location of a community, while one's commitment and passion can have a much broader reach.

Black men must lead in demonstrating that giving our youth much of what we did not have is not as important as giving them what we did have—a work ethic, a sense of purpose, a commitment to never give up, and the discipline to think before acting.

Black men must assist the Black male in developing an analytical ability to solve the many challenges he will undoubtedly face on life's journey. Succinctly, the Black male must know what game he is in, the rules of the game, and how to use the rules to win. Metaphorically, I share with Black males: "If you show up to the basketball game dressed in a football helmet, shoulder pads, and cleats, you cannot get mad with the coach for not putting you in the game. You are not dressed to play."

In communities where we live and work, Black men must strive to be the difference we seek. Within the five basic institutions of society (family, economic, education, religious, and government), the Black man's effective presence and contributions will continue to be crucial in the positive development and growth of humanity. Solving the puzzle of life requires that we must share hindsight (understanding of past experiences), insight (understanding of present conditions) and foresight (the ability to look ahead and craft a forward direction). Black men must amplify that hindsight + insight + foresight = vision on life's journey. Without vision, a people will perish.

Black men must be bridge builders for the Black males who would otherwise have the singular path of wading in the deep waters of negative outcomes. I urge Black men to build the bridges and assist the Black males in clearing other paths and scaling the economic and educational mountains to come.

Black men sharing their respective lessons learned on their journeys will contribute to the Black males becoming strong Black men, and in turn strong husbands, fathers, and mentors for future generations.

Dr. Andrew A. Ray
39th Grand Basileus of Omega Psi Phi Fraternity, Inc.

PREFACE

In the United States, it has been routinely highlighted that millions of Black children live in a home without the physical presence of a father and that many fathers who are present in the home are not emotionally available. For decades, the public dialogue has emphasized the negative impact of absent fathers, and the larger discussions have projected an overwhelming negative image of Black men. Fatherlessness is a national emergency, worthy of being an epidemic, because the narrative has been that fatherlessness is associated with the socio-ecological risks facing our children. The negative impact of not having a father present shows up not only in homes, but also in schools, prisons, and the streets.

It's been a long time coming, but the Black Lives Matter Movement has raised a universal call for African Americans to change the narrative for Black fathers. This book highlights not only Black fathers who are present in the lives of their own children, but who have served as surrogates for their younger siblings, stepchildren, grandchildren, nephews, nieces, and even mentees. These are only a few untold stories, but there are countless stories in our community that the media does not highlight.

The intention of sharing the stories of these fathers is to illuminate that Black men do take care of their children and to encourage fathers that despite the struggles of being a single parent, lack of finances, and health issues, your children still need your physical and emotional presence. Changing the narrative for Black fathers has implications for the positive development of Black children and is essential for the positive well-being of families and youth in general. The results of Black men being involved include but are not limited to improved behavioral, academic, and health outcomes for their children.

REFLECTIONS

Frederick C. Hinnant

In the world in which we live, one thing is crystal clear.
There is no way without a father could we have gotten here.

Traveling life's perilous paths is impossible without another chosen for such a remedial task—a father and a mother searching the word of God for the answer I found from Genesis to Revelation—it was spreading like cancer.

Providing life and sound advice is fruitful in every way,
Strong affection and protection, keeping enemies at bay.

Breaking the fallow grounds of life for seed later to be sown,
Trusting God without a doubt for everything unknown.

Allowing proper room for growth whenever it is needed,
Never neglecting chastisement, so every word is heeded.

Love has him clear the path of life so that you will not stumble,
Walking with wisdom along the trail, exalted yet very humble.

Inculcating spiritual morals and values written in stone,
Saturating the mind and heart, quickened through tissue
and bone.

This is the calling of our fathers to love, to protect, and to provide.
Tis the vocation of his children to love and instruction abide.

A family without a father is like the cake without the batter.
Void the thought—it is plain to see that fathers really matter.

FATHERHOOD: FROM PLEASURE TO PAIN TO PEACE

Anthony J. McAllister

Fatherhood is ordained by God and is a journey that will lead you down different expressways in life. Whether you are a biological father, stepfather, or mentor, it is paramount that you allow God to order your steps. While Merriam-Webster defines a father as a male parent or a man who begets a child, I learned much about the definition of a father from my own father, the late Elder Theodore James McAllister Sr.

As a youth, I experienced my father not being big on public display of affection. I believe this trait to be characteristic of men of my father's generation. I always felt genuinely loved through their care and provisions for me. This set the stage for how I would ultimately parent and care for my children.

As a boy, I wanted to emulate and please my father in every way possible. He was what I call a man among men. When he married my mother, the late Mrs. Sallie Lyon McAllister, they united in marriage with eight children each. As if this was not enough, they added my brother and me to their union, adopted a grandson, and became legal guardian of two other grandchildren. Grandchildren were always present in our household, being nurtured by my parents. I followed my parents' example and became a mentor to my nieces and nephews, and today I am embraced as "Beloved."

Early on, my parents embraced Joshua's house rule: "As for me and my house, we will serve the Lord" (Joshua 24:15, KJV). They taught us and modeled how we were to love God and love each other. The strange yet beautiful thing about my family was that I never heard any sibling refer to each other or my father or mother as "step." I recall my mother's children always having such a beautiful relationship with my father, and the same with my father's children relative to my mother. While all my siblings were not living under the same roof simultaneously, our family gatherings produced lots of food, fun, and fellowship. The blending of these two families and the evolving loving relationships that impacted my life significantly, as I would emulate these personas in adulthood.

God gifted me with the ability to excel in baseball. During my senior year in high school, I received an invitation to "try out" with the Pittsburgh Pirates. My high school Baccalaureate Service was scheduled on the same date. I did not want to miss this celebratory Baccalaureate event with my classmates. My parents allowed me to make the decision. I skipped the professional baseball tryouts. I often ask myself whether my parents and I made a mistake or not. I am blessed that my ability to play baseball afforded full scholarships for the duration of my college years. I graduated from Saint Augustine's College in Raleigh, North Carolina in 1988, and shortly after that, in 1989, moved to Maryland, where I would reside with my sister Rev. Lillie I. Sanders.

In 1992, I was blessed to marry the love of my life, Tyreese Woulard, whom I met while we were in college. She was a student at Shaw University in Raleigh, North Carolina. Although it would be years before we would have our own child, I emulated my father by embracing various opportunities to act in the role of father figure. While working with the Northern Virginia Urban League as a youth specialist from 1990 to 1992, I mentored three young men. I am blessed that the young men continue to be a part of my life.

Continuing in my father's parenting footsteps, my wife and I took on the role of parenting her cousin Andre from the time he was twelve through his completion of high school. This afforded me additional experience up close in preparation for fatherhood. I have watched these young men become husbands, fathers, and productive members of society. They often share their appreciation for my being a great example of what a father figure should be.

While I always desired to be a father, my career-oriented wife was not anxious to experience the pains of childbirth. She even toyed with the idea of adoption, yet she honored me with two beautiful daughters. During our journey to parenthood, my wife had a miscarriage which left us heartbroken. On May 13, 1997, my fatherhood journey began with the birth of my first beautiful daughter, N'daja Lyndze McAllister. Daja, as we affectionately call her, graced the world's stage and hit the ground running. She was a naturally smart child who moved to her own beat. She seemed to always be on the "catch me if you can move," laughing every step of the way. Daja amazed us as she began reading at an early age. As a young child, Daja had a natural compassion for everyone. She conquered childhood milestones with ease, almost as if she were moving aside, making room for her baby sister.

While in my first year of navigating the fatherhood role, the thirteenth month blessed us with another daughter, Ayana, on June 10, 1998. Ayana Jazmyn McAllister graced our lives with her presence. While she was our baby, Daja reminded everyone that Ayana was her baby, whom she protected and taught to tie her shoelaces.

I thank God for allowing my wife and me to be co-laborers with Him in bringing our girls into the world. In appreciation and obedience, my wife and I mold our daughters to be responsible, kind, beautiful, and respectful young ladies. Watching Ayana and Daja blossom into such beautiful flowers was such a moving and gratifying experience for me.

As a young father, I remember the pride I felt when my girls excitedly greeted me when I came home from work. This made me feel like a superhero. However, through their early education and our faith, they got to know the real Superhero—God, the Father. The girls needed to receive the best education possible. We enrolled them in Catholic and Christian schools. I remember driving my girls to school and singing with them songs from a Sesame Street cassette. One of our favorite songs was *Put Down the Duckie*. This song and other songs from the cassette would be our morning sing-along ritual. Their school curriculum and our Christian faith allowed them to want to know more about God. We kept Ayana and Daja in worship and church-related activities. At an early age, they asked to be baptized. My wife and I find comfort in knowing that our girls truly learned to love the Lord.

As the girls became interested in cheerleading, I quickly became a "girl dad" long before the phrase became popular. No matter what the activity was, if my girls were involved, you saw me! When the girls were in middle school, I watched with amazement as my babies were growing into young adults. I remember the time I proudly escorted both girls to a father-daughter ball. What a beautiful event it was, and a wonderful time spent with dad and daughters.

From middle school to high school came the interest of boys. What a "girl dad" nightmare! Their high school years were exciting times. My girls were in their element, becoming social butterflies. My wife and I welcomed many of their friends into our home. We enjoyed every aspect of encouraging these teens to prepare themselves for the next stages in their lives.

Both girls graduated from high school, and in 2016, I was proud when both girls entered St. Augustine's University in Raleigh, North Carolina—my alma mater. Off to college was an exciting time in our household, as my wife and I had worked hard to prepare our girls for college. We were happy that they were attending a historically Black college and university (HBCU).

What joy, pride, and excitement we all had the first year. As a family, we attended our first HBCU homecoming on the campus of St. Augustine's University. That homecoming day was filled with pride as I introduced my wife and daughters to friends I had known for more than twenty-five years. I watched as my girls proudly introduced their friends to all of their uncles, many of whom happened to be my Omega Psi Phi Fraternity brothers. This excitement would only grow as we anticipated attending homecomings together for the next three years.

This anticipated excitement would come to a screeching halt on the evening of March 20, 2017—a day that will forever be etched in my mind, my heart, and my soul. You see, this was the day I lost my precious baby girl, Ayana, to gun violence. I would never see her alive again. I would never experience her doting love on me as "Daddy's baby."

When Ayana was born, I had the same feeling I had when my first daughter N'daja was born. My number one prayer for each daughter was for a healthy birth. When I laid eyes on Ayana, I knew she would be special. Something about being a father to girls makes the world right from a man's perspective. Early in, I vowed to always be a "girl dad" to my daughters. It was God's purpose and my pleasure.

The normal course of life is that children bury their parents.

Death was not new to me as I had lost my mother, my father, a sister. Additionally, I lost three brothers and a nephew, who were victims of gun violence. Yet nothing in life prepared me for the loss of a child, especially my beautiful baby daughter, who was in her first year of college and home on spring break. It has been said that death is traumatic if it comes without warning, is untimely, or involves violence. These occurrences clearly define how I continue to feel losing my beloved Ayana.

As men, we are taught to be strong and not to show our true emotions. I held fast to all of this in the days, months, and years after losing my daughter. I struggled from day to day with my feelings. You see, from one day to the next, I never knew which emotion would show up. There were times when I felt angry and lost, and other times, I was an emotional wreck. Dads are supposed to be their children's protectors. There were times I felt like a total failure in that regard. While dealing with these emotions privately, I never let go of my faith in God or my faith community.

The Bible states in Proverbs 22:6 (KJV), "Train up a child in the way he should go: and when he is old, he will not depart from it." I honor my parents' obedience to this Scripture, for it taught me the importance of staying connected to the Vine. I witnessed both parents lose children to death. They both held onto their faith and found comfort in the promises of God's Word: "Fear not, for I am with you; be not dismayed, for I am your God; I will strengthen you, I will help you, I will uphold you with my righteous right hand" (Isaiah 41:10, ESV). These promises continue to be a comfort to me.

Another aspect of my healing has been therapy. Like most African Americans, I was reluctant to seek therapy because of the stigma attached to it. With the impact of this personal tragedy, I knew that I needed to prepare myself for what might come later. Therapy allows me to engage my inner feelings, fully understand the different stages of the grief process, and know that people grieve differently. My sessions with my therapist are invaluable. To my brothers everywhere, whatever life brings your way, do not be afraid to try therapy.

Fatherhood is a journey that will lead us down different paths. Whether you are a biological father, stepfather, or a mentor, allow God to order your steps. I am grateful for every opportunity God has allowed me to pour into the lives of young men who were without the presence of a present father.

God's grace allowed my wife and me to be co-laborers with Him in the lives of our two daughters. Oh God, how I deeply miss Ayana, yet, I hold fast to the sweet memories of watching her blossom into a beautiful young lady during her eighteen years on earth. I am comforted in knowing that her unshakeable love for God and humanity ushered her into the Kingdom.

While her murder case remains unsolved, I am at peace, for I have submitted to God's Word in Romans 12:17a (NIV): "Do not repay anyone evil for evil." and 19 (NIV): "Do not take revenge, my dear friends, but leave room for God's wrath, for it is written: 'It is mine to avenge; I will repay,' says the LORD." People often make the comment, "Man, I don't know how you can be so strong." My reply is, "This tragedy has truly shown me that I have more of the Spirit of God in me than even I realized." In loving memory of Ayana, the Ayana J. McAllister Legacy Foundation was birthed. The mission of the Ayana J. McAllister Legacy Foundation is to deliberately engage communities of color disproportionately impacted by gun violence through advocacy and educational strategies. The foundation has provided scholarship money to deserving high school graduates. Additionally, we pray that through this foundation, incidents of homicide, suicide, and acts of violence resulting from the irresponsible use of firearms by high-risk individuals will be significantly reduced.

On March 21, 2018, the community where Ayana was killed—Fort Chaplin in Washington, DC—honored Ayana's memory by naming a wing in their new state-of-the-art Community Center, the Ayana J. McAllister Education Center. Ayana's eighteen years on earth touched a multitude of people in so many ways. Ayana's living was not in vain. To God, be the glory.

Our beloved daughter, N'daja Lyndze McAllister, has blessed us with a beloved grandson, Zyir, who fills our hearts with love and hope.

"Therefore, I say to all the fathers reading this chapter, "Fatherhood: From Pleasure to Pain to Peace," love your children. Be present, be a provider, be a protector, be a promise keeper, and keep them prayed up. This, my friends, will be an earthly investment in which you will draw heavenly dividends, for now, and for eternity.

RULES TO DAD BY

John Bannister, PhD

Before I give my two cents on fatherhood, I wanted to tell a little about myself. Looking back, I don't have many complaints about my younger years. Although I grew up in a single-parent home, my mother, older sister, and I formed a cohesive unit that allowed us to stay out of trouble and move forward. Like many of the young men with whom I grew up, I had limited contact with my father as a youth. Those close to me know that I only remember seeing my dad twice, the later instance was at his funeral when I was eight. I can remember my mom getting the phone call one Sunday morning and having to tell me that my daddy was gone. I remember eating eggs and watching a Jets game on a thirteen-inch black-and-white TV in our kitchen in Marcy Projects. I can remember the design in the fork I was using the moment I found out my father was deceased more than I can remember any interactions with him. Sounds sad, right? There was a stretch of my childhood where I harbored a great deal of anger toward him for not being there. Ironically, that resentment started at eight years old and lasted until about 17, all after he died. But being honest, teenage John would spend the majority of this writing airing out how he felt not having a connection that should have been there. As a husband and a father, I have long put that anger behind me. However, the man in me will never forgive him for leaving my mother and sister.

I finished high school something like 267th out of 512 students, pretty much an average student. To this day, I think about what could have been if I would have applied myself more during those formative years. I was definitely what most would consider a late bloomer. Although I went off to college right after high school, I was in my late twenties when I finally decided that it was important for me to finish a degree. I then went on to spend the better part of a decade going from not having a degree at all to being a PhD. To date, the proudest moment of my life was getting my PhD and having my family present for that, particularly my son, Joshua. Josh is currently thirteen, lives in a house with parents with advanced degrees, and is mandated to do better than us.

I use the two anecdotes above to give you a guidepost to my approach to fatherhood. In all honesty, they describe every bit of nervousness, fear, and concern I have ever had about being a dad. They have also provided me with a base from which to pull in ensuring that I put my best foot forward for my son. I believe fatherhood requires presence and the desire and ability to be way more than average every day. As a father, your presence has to be maintained in your child's life and should be developed even if you cannot always be there physically. The requirement to pursue more than just an average existence is just as vital as you set the groundwork for your son or daughter's outlook on growth. I will provide more insight on these two concepts below.

Presence

If I could advise any father, I would start by telling them to make every effort to be there for their child. A dad being present in a child's life, especially a Black child's, is likely the absolute best thing a father can do. While I cannot present any real research on this, I know that I am driven to be present in my son's life as much as possible. I made that promise to him well before he was born.

Maintaining presence is more profound than being fiscally responsible for a child. Money is necessary, but time is also required. The benefit of being an active participant in your child's life will outweigh anything you buy. And purely from the perspective of someone who grew up without that connection to my dad, any money he may have contributed to my upbringing did not make enough difference to make up for him not being there. I firmly believe that given the choice, most of us would choose a father's presence over anything else.

Two songs released in the early 2000s by Beanie Sigel and Jay-Z perfectly capture the feeling of growing up without a father's presence. More than the actual lyrics, these two songs released across separate albums allow these MCs to share their anger that stemmed from their dads not being there (*Where Have You Been*) and the desire to repair these fractured relationships (*I Still Got Love for You*). I have always felt the pain in Beanie's voice when he talks about being kicked out the house because he looked like his dad and the pain and sadness Jay had to feel when he rhymed:

> *Your lack of love left me loveless, and I'm of your breath*
> *I'm your mind, body, and soul, your heart, your flesh*
> *Your alcohol, your smoke, it results in a mess*
> *And Dad, still I love you no less, Dad*
> *Hope you didn't think success would make me less mad*
> *But not mad, just disappointed, we wasted years*

As a dad, being away from my son for an extended period of time is always tough on me, and it will always be compounded by my own feelings. While life has dealt me few regrets, there was a time in which circumstances led to me having a limited presence in my son's life, which will always haunt me. When Josh was seven, I took a position in Florida that was a great move for my career. At the time, I was looking to grow as a person and a leader as well as a dad. I wanted to be able to provide more for my family, and I realized that in order to accelerate that growth, I had to step out on faith. While the opportunity provided career growth, it was not a role that merited uprooting and relocating my family, as my wife was firmly secured in her career and we are blessed to have a stable village to support

Josh. We decided that I would take the role and reassess after a year if it merited a total relocation. This was the toughest time in my life. Over five years later, I still kick myself for not being as present as I should have been for Josh. I feel like I missed a chunk of formative time with him and pray daily that this time has been made up. We were blessed to create some incredible memories during the times he came to visit and even more after I transitioned back to Charlotte, but I spent many sleepless nights thinking about the well-being of my son and my lack of presence during this time.

Presence does not mean that you have to stay in a relationship that is not healthy. I am blessed to be coming up on two decades of marriage, and I know several fathers who make it work with their "baby mommas." You will encounter stressful situations at times, but you have to ensure that your child knows you are there for them. There is no textbook on this—no roadmap to follow to get this right. Unfortunately, much of the messaging on Black fatherhood encourages a negative cycle.

I have always asked myself why the media pushes stories of Black people growing up without contact with their fathers. You always get stories about star athletes growing up fatherless, but you rarely hear about the contributions of dads in the lives of these stars. What about Richard Williams (Venus and Serena), Earl Woods (Tiger) and Matthew Knowles (Beyoncé)? The narrative about these three fathers quickly moved from the role they played in their children's lives to them not being there. I know this may sound like a conspiracy theory, but I challenge you to read the Wikipedia pages of these dads. You tell me if it feels like something is missing. Interestingly, the media did not seem to have a problem promoting Lavar Ball, who, to his credit, has created a brand with his three talented sons but seems to be driven more by the allure of celebrity.

I hope that, as Black fathers, we can start to control the narrative on our role. This work is a start. I am sharing my thoughts on fatherhood as you should, and I remain committed to both the role of a dad and the story we can craft. For me, maintaining a presence in my child's life is the most important message I can share.

More than Average

If I do my job right as a dad, my son will be a better version of me. I remember when my wife and I were thinking of names for our soon-to-be-born baby. She really wanted to name him John Jr., and I was totally against it. My logic was two-fold. First, I am a Junior, and everything in me was against naming my son after my father. His role in my life did not merit or deserve that reward, period. Second, I wanted my son to walk his own path as much as possible. To me, he deserved the right to be his own person as much as possible, and being named after me could stand in the way of that. While I know she did not agree with me on either count, my wife eventually conceded to me with this request, and the name Joshua came to her in a dream.

While Josh is expected to walk his own path, it is my job to help guide him. With that stated, my expectations for him are higher than the expectations I have for myself. I will never let him settle for just enough. He is not allowed to do the bare minimum. It is completely unacceptable for him to be average. Some will say there is nothing wrong with being average. And to be honest, I can almost agree with that. But not for him. I will always push him to be more, even when it is not fun. Because in every average person you come across, myself included, you also meet someone capable of more. Part of my purpose as a dad is to push him toward more and be okay with him not liking it.

There is an essential requirement in setting a high bar for your offspring, which is that you must live to the same standards. Do not expect more from your child than you do from yourself. If you want your child to be great, you have to be putting forth every effort to be just as great as you expect them to be.

It is likely that many of the authors in this book grew up hearing the phrase "Do as I say and not as I do." For such a short phrase, it always seemed that a large volume of information is loaded into it. When my mom said it, it often meant that if I did not adhere to her "request," the consequences would not be pleasant. In today's world, this statement likely holds the same meaning, but in a world where children have had access to so much knowledge through what they see (television, the internet, social media), it's so much easier for a kid to copy what they see than to chart their own path. Like it or not, we must compete for the development of our children's mindset with good and bad from all over the planet. If you are not willing to provide a mirror for them to look at that shows a constant pursuit of growth and a desire to be better, chances are the playlist they choose to follow throughout their life could only provide insight on just getting by. Set the example of greatness by always striving for greatness yourself because they are always watching.

If you, like me, settled for average for even a portion of your life, how do you lead your child toward desiring more? Even if you maintain a life of overachievement, how do you stoke that fire in a child who could have likely been handed these advantages? The honest answer is that you find a way. I cannot say I have a set of strategies that will always work. And I will caution you not to take that kind of advice. What I will suggest is that you watch, listen, and react to your child. When you understand what your child needs, you provide it. It may be tough love, or it may be space, or likely some combination of both. As a dad, your job is to figure it out so you can help them do the same. The better you get at it—and if you try, you will get better—the better you will do.

Summary

Life has a way of making wrong moments right, at least from the things you learn from them. The lessons learned from my lack of contact with my father and the length of time I spent being average influence every single breath I breathe in parenthood. God has blessed me with a son, allowing me the opportunity to assess and reassess the steps I made in life, challenging me to do better in his. As a father, be present and be okay with guiding your child to be great. Never let them settle for average. And never settle for just being an average father.

NEW BEGINNING

Emmett Burke

As a new father of a seven-month-old girl, I am continuing to learn something new every day. I am blessed to have a strong woman as my wife and the mother of my daughter, much like my mother and aunt growing up. My father was present my entire childhood and is still a significant part of my success and support system to this day. Many of my peers in my community were without their fathers, and my father was also a father figure in their lives. He was a role model, a source of support and information, and a great example of man to many of my friends.

At a young age, I realized that I was truly blessed and vowed to mature into an honorable man like my father. His reliability, work ethic, confidence, disposition, and intelligence continue to inspire and motivate me. I learned not to take my father's presence for granted, as many of my peers did not have their fathers in their lives. I saw certain behaviors and decisions made by some of my friends growing up that sometimes confused me. As I got older, I realized that my father's behavior naturally rubbed off on me and my younger brother and helped us climb the ladder of life's success and meet challenges with poise and strategy. From goal setting to life planning, my father influenced it all in my life. My father lost his father at the age of ten and his stepfather at the age of fourteen. He spent several days and nights telling us stories about these traumatic experiences and how they impacted him as an adult. Despite the tremendous amount of grief he experienced as a young boy, he explained to us that it made him grow up fast and step into manhood quickly yet unprepared. My father is my example of what a man is and what a great father is.

Throughout my new and very brief parenting journey, my wife and my family have been a consistent resource for me. I am still learning how to be the best I can be as a father and how to also be a supportive husband to my wife. I am learning that her happiness and satisfaction have a significant impact on my parenting experience. As great as it sounds to think it's all about the child, a part of fatherhood and parenting that no one told me about was collaborating, compromising, and adjusting with the mother. Caring for the mother is just as important as caring for your child. It's her child too, and you may not always agree.

In closing, fatherhood will not be the same for every man, but hopefully it's a joyful experience. The challenges and the long nights are worth it when you see the joy you bring to your child's eyes. I continue to learn every day and hope to have more children in the future.

GOD AT WORK

Rev. Dr. Robert Cheeks Jr.

Throughout my life's journey, I've had the privilege of adorning a number of nicknames. Thankfully, only a couple have stayed with me to this day. If it's not my family name, "Cheeks," then it's "six-four." Since the first day we met, just over twenty years ago, my wife has affectionately called me by my height, 6'4". While she was impressed with my height, my family had other expectations in mind. Not only was my family excited about our union, but they were equally anticipating the offspring of our union. We were looking forward to adding to the family, too. We love kids. I am often considered a "kid at heart." I love to laugh, crack jokes, and enjoy every moment, especially when it comes to the children connected to us. I love people. In fact, pouring into people is what I do. I serve as a Senior Pastor. My years of serving in ministry have stretched the length of our union. Just like our family, our church family couldn't wait to welcome the little Cheekses. I couldn't wait either. I've watched and admired the joy of having children brought to my family and friends. The moment for us to expand our family could not come quick enough.

It has always been my understanding that the natural progression of a romantic relationship that leads to marriage is the expanding of the family. If children do not already exist, having a child after marriage is something mostly all newlyweds consider as the next step. Some plan for it, while others just let it happen whenever it happens. Then there are those for whom it never happens. They plan for pregnancy, they agree the time is right, but nothing ever happens. I never imagined in all of my life that that would be me. The thought never entered my mind. In my estimation, it was supposed to happen after marrying my wife and after making plans. But it never happened. I figured, just like everybody else, that one day we would move right into procreation.

Unfortunately, that day never came. It did not happen when we wanted it to happen. It did not happen when we did not plan for it to happen. It simply never happened. Nope. Nothing. After twenty years of holy matrimony, we have never given birth to a child. Now, at this point, you're probably wondering how am I writing about being a father if I've never had a child. Having read this far, I would raise the same question. How in the world are you contributing to work for fathers if you've never experienced procreation? Well, you've raised a question that I have yet to comprehend fully. I am still in awe of being considered to raise a child from birth.

The same feeling I had two years ago is exactly what I feel right now. I am completely floored by it all. The day we were asked to fully parent an unborn child during the third month of the mother's pregnancy was mind-blowing. Being asked by two incredible people to share this story from a father's perspective is mind-blowing. I am truly humbled and honored by both. All of it has caused me to deeply ponder what the Lord has done and is doing. Everything that has happened in my life, particularly within this part of my life, is evidence that God is real. Like the bright yellow signs on a construction site that read "Caution: Men & women at work," my life's sign reads "God at work." When having kids did not happen, God was working. When my wife and I felt like we were forgotten, God was working. While enduring the pain of isolation, God was working. When I accepted this as our plight and felt that we would be without child for the rest of our lives, God was working. As the saying goes, "God may not come when you want Him to, but He's always right on time." No matter what happens, God is always at work.

Very early during my faith journey, I learned that God does not operate according to our timetable. We cannot dictate God. We cannot command God to do what we want God to do. God is God, and God all by God's self. In view of the sovereignty of God, I learned to believe God, trust God, and serve God. I love God. If living for God were a sport, I'd be a starter for "Team Jesus." In all seriousness, I'm not claiming to be a super-saint or spiritual elitist. I am certainly not an angel or cherub. I am far from being perfect. It's just that with all the years of walking with God, I never saw infertility and adoption as my assignment. My current assignment as a senior pastor was obvious. It was clear that God prepared me over the years to serve an amazing group of people. However, the assignment of both husband and wife being medically cleared with no reason as to why we were without child was nowhere in view.

I never saw this coming. I know we do not possess powers to see and know what God is up to before God reveals it to us. I do not think this wasn't supposed to happen to us or that God owed us a child. No, that's not what this is about. Even though God did command Adam and Eve to be fruitful and to multiply, this was not what God had in mind for us. When God is at work and that work intersects at a particular juncture in our lives, we must surrender to the fulfillment of destiny when it arrives. Did I know this was my destiny? Did I know that at the age of forty-five, with seventeen years of marriage now a part of history, that we would have a baby without ever being pregnant? No, I did not. I was solely focused on serving my wife, my family, and God's people. Often, God waits for us to fall completely asleep in Him before blowing our minds. Like Adam, before having a rib extracted from his side to receive a major gift from God, most of us do not realize that God adds to our lives when we're completely resting in God.

For years, I have been resting in God, or so I thought. The void was still there. By the grace of God, I excelled in the work of ministry, received many opportunities at growth and development, and earned various degrees, but was still without child. I've been very fortunate to be in the ministry for twenty years, in which I've had the privilege and honor to pastor a church for thirteen. A senior pastor's role is often considered as a "spiritual-parent"—someone who God has placed in our lives for our spiritual well-being. Some have equated me to the likes of an actual father. The comparisons are strikingly similar, but not having children is not a requirement to be a pastor. If I had a dollar for the many times I've heard focusing on my pastorate is the reason why we do not have children, I would have enough resources to franchise a couple of Chick-fil-As. If we had a baby to match the number of times that other women automatically assumed my wife had health challenges and not me, we would have co-starred in the next multiple reality TV shows for several seasons.

Dealing with insensitivity toward infertility is very discouraging at times. There are hundreds of other pastors who have had children and can focus on their pastorate successfully, yet I'm the one who has to focus without. I'm the rarity. I am not the norm. I am stigmatized, which is upsetting at times. However, for the sake of God's goodness, I'm used to maintaining my witness and chalk it up as a misunderstanding. The unintentional yet painful things people say and do are too much to spend time dealing with here. Besides, I make mistakes, too. Before becoming a father, I was no longer desensitized to the pain that infertility brings to a family. For instance, we were not considered a family until we had a child.

Once our son arrived, people started referring to us as "the family." So what were we before? I thought we were always a family. Maybe I'm wrong, but being on the other side of this has opened me up to the other areas of life that many have ignored, including myself.

I have operated with implicit biases toward infertility and didn't even know it. Infertility is a reality that sometimes Blacks endure all by themselves. Instead of finding support and encouragement from our community, our community seems to think this concern doesn't exist. I couldn't sit idly by and act like just because we had healthy reproductive systems that we were exempt from not having a child. We have yet to produce a child. So instead of ignoring this and acting like we were okay, I seized the opportunity to minister to other husbands or men in relationships experiencing infertility. I discovered that most of these brothers chose not to move their relationships toward marriage or to dissolve their marriage solely for this reason. I couldn't comprehend this. I married my wife for her, not a child. This wasn't a deal breaker for me. To me, the possibilities of having a child were up to God. It was according to God's plan for us. I just never considered it coming by way of adoption.

Consequently, I believe this is why I'm here—not only to add to the number of men who've selflessly given themselves to raising a child in need, but also to encourage you to do the same. I want to inspire you just like others have done for me. There are countless numbers of other African Americans who are blessed through the process of adoption. My grandparents fostered and adopted. We have extended family and friends who have adopted or been adopted. Even though I've been recently included in the number of adoptive parents, this is nothing new to us as a people. Blacks have been taking in family and friends since the days the systems and practices of slavery destroyed the Black family construct. Parents have had to raise their children's children. Aunts and uncles have had to raise their nieces and nephews. Whether through guardianship or adoption, great sacrifices to maintain the family have passed down from generation to generation. We've been rebuilding the Black family for decades. This is who we are. It is in our blood. And I'm honored to be a part of our legacy. This is God's assignment for my life, and maybe yours.

Perhaps this is God's assignment for you. I hope that sharing my story has encouraged you. If you're reading this and you are wrestling with whether you should leave or stay in the relationship, know that God is at work. If you and your significant other are contemplating adoption or becoming foster parents, this story has been divinely crafted just for you. Pray and ask God if this is what God has for you. The one prayer that directed my wife and me to this life-changing moment was simple and plain. It came from a Bible study that I led one night at the church. In his book, *Experiencing God,* Henry Blackaby said, "God, please show me where You're working and invite me to join You there." And God did. God showed me through one phone call how I was to become a father. Maybe this is the answered prayer you've been waiting for. Maybe you're connected to someone who needs to hear this. You could be the blessing for which someone has prayed.

It is my aim to help. My father, affectionately known as the "General," instilled in me the importance of helping others. My father-in-love, affectionately known as "Big-Red," used to remind me that there's always someone less fortunate who could use your assistance. Both served this country, fought in several wars, and retired from successful military careers in the Army. Both are leaders. They possess incredible leadership skills. They are highly regarded within their professional context and within the communities in which they live. They make us feel loved. We love them dearly. I mention them because I am grateful for their examples of great sacrifice, and more importantly, their examples of fatherhood. My dad taught me to live life in a manner that makes life better for others. Because of him, serving for the betterment of others is my life's mission. Little did I know this would include my own son. The Lord once told Paul that "it is better to give than to receive." The world system teaches us in order to get, you take. Jesus teaches us in order to get, you give. I've learned that when you're a blessing, you eventually set yourself up to receive a blessing. My son is a major blessing. I'm blessed to be his father. There are others who long to experience what my son now has. A father. I pray you allow God to do the same through you.

The saying has it that God works in mysterious ways. To me, God just works. His ways aren't mysterious to Him. I recognize that this work did not have to be. Yet, God gave me the chance to be a father! I will never take this privilege for granted.

My blood or not, he is my son, and I am his father.

DAD ON THE REBOUND: PARENTING WHILE INCARCERATED

George E. Coker

"Blessed is he whose transgression is forgiven, whose sin is covered. Blessed is the man unto whom the LORD imputeth not iniquity, and in whose spirit there is no guile."

—Psalm 32:1-2, KJV

Growing up as a young child, I always wondered what it would feel like having my dad around to do things with me. Now do not get me wrong, my father was always there in the physical aspects of my life, but I desperately needed my dad as well to nurture and spend some quality time with his son. I never felt wanted by my dad while growing up, and I vowed to myself that if I ever became a parent, I would always be there for my children and do the necessary things with them and for them so that they would always feel loved and wanted, never neglected. To mask the pain I was feeling inside for my dad not being there for me, I started playing sports. It didn't matter which sport I played. I just wanted to escape the longing of my dad not spending any time with me. The fortunate thing for me about getting involved with sports is that it allowed me to have several "dads" in my life who were hands-on and taught me valuable life lessons through sports that I still carry with me today. I embraced all of the teaching methods that my coaches, teachers, and older men in my community bestowed upon me while growing up and implemented them in my daily life so that I could become a better dad to my children.

Fast forward to November 4, 1990, when my life as a second-semester junior at Shaw University, a father of two small children, and a recently engaged man changed forever. I committed a crime of murder against a female friend of mine, which laid me in prison with a life sentence (eligible for parole at twenty years) that I am still currently serving. As I sat in jail waiting to be sentenced, there were two things weighing heavy on my mind—the remorse I felt from taking a life and the regret in knowing that I wouldn't be out there to raise my three children, Jurica, Arsenio, and Jasmine. (Jasmine is not my biological daughter, but I've been in her life since she was two, and I'm the only "dad" she knows.) When I went to prison, being a parent to my children was the furthest thing from my mind, not because I didn't want to, but because I didn't know how to be a parent to my children while being away from them.

Over the years during my incarceration, I have maintained a great relationship with my children, and that's a testament to their mothers, Kecia, Nada, and Phyllis. They have allowed me to be a parent to my children in every sense of the word. Now that is not saying that my children and I haven't had our disagreements along the way, but as a parent, you must be stern in your convictions by letting them know that just because you're not out there with them, you're still the parent, and they are the child.

Example 1: There were times when I had to discipline my children by putting them on punishment for not following the rules that their mothers and I set forth for them. Was it an easy thing to do in here? No. But it was necessary at the time. As a parent, you can't allow a child to defy you in any way, shape, or form, because if you do, they will lose their respect for you, and once that happens, it's hard to get it back.

Example 2: One time, my two older sisters came down from Philadelphia to visit. While they were here, they went and picked up my older daughter, Jurica, who was twelve years old at the time, to come along for a visit. While we were all visiting one another, I got on my daughter's case for not answering my letters and keeping in touch with me. Now granted, at the time, I was a little harsh with my baby girl, but I felt that she needed to understand where I was coming from. She didn't like the way I was talking to her, so she just shut down and started crying and didn't speak to me for the rest of the visit. I, in turn, told her that if she didn't want to come and see me on her own volition, she didn't have to. And guess what she did? She did not come and see me again until she was a senior in college.

During the years that I did not see my daughter, we still kept in touch regularly via letters and phone calls, but I learned a valuable lesson that day in parenting. Because of my selfishness of wanting what I wanted and not asking my daughter what she wanted, I created a problem that I had to fix. So, I wrote to my daughter and apologized to her for my actions. Being away from your children is no easy feat, and parenting them from a distance is even a bigger challenge in itself. At the same time, learn to listen to your children and understand their feelings and what they are going through. Learning to do this helped us mend our father-daughter relationship. Let that be a lesson learned that we as parents don't always get it right and that we still have a lot to learn about parenting our children whether we are out there with them or away from them.

Below are what I feel are necessary tools in helping men such as ourselves stay relevant in our children's lives:

- ❯ You must have an open dialogue with your children's mother, because it is not about you and her. It's all about the child's well-being.

- ❯ Stay in touch with your children regularly via letters, cards, phone calls, and visits, but only if they are allowed to and if they want to see you. Please do not force yourself on them. The most important rule is to always open with "Dad loves you and misses you." This is a must, and it's not up for debate no matter what.

❯ Whenever you and their mother decide the time is right, tell your children what you did to take you away from them, but don't go into details unless you both feel as though they are mature enough to understand this information.

❯ Whenever you reach out to your children by using these methods, always ask them pertinent questions about their daily activities. It's important that they feel loved and wanted at all times.

❯ At no time when you are engaging your children in conversation should you ask about what their mother has been doing or who she is seeing, because it's not about you. It's all about the children.

❯ Don't make promises that you know you can't keep. Just be open and honest with them and keep it real at all times.

❯ When speaking with your children on the phone, make sure that you spend at least 95 percent of your allotted time talking with them and not their mother or guardian.

❯ Whatever methods that you choose to use in parenting your children while you're away from them, just make sure that they're genuine, because a child can sense if you are not sincere with their feelings.

In 2007, I was blessed to become a grandparent for the first time to a beautiful princess by the name of Ta'saya. Since then, my children have given me three more grandchildren—Liam, Ava and Chase—whom I love and adore mightily. They are the reason why I'm still going strong today, even though I've yet to meet them. I've implemented the same parenting methods to my grandchildren as I did my children many years ago.

As incarcerated men, we still have an obligation to be there for our children and grandchildren. As parents, just because we are not physically able to be out there with them, we can still be a positive influence in their lives and nurture them to the best of our abilities.

PRINCIPLES OF FATHERHOOD

Dionta L. Douglas

One day, it was brought to my attention how each father's commitment to family impacts the overall foundation and growth of today's leaders and tomorrow's visionaries in our communities. When the question of how important fathers are was asked of me, I had to look back over my own life to better understand how we as men resonate in the eyes of the people we lead. Growing up in an African American community in the late 1970s through 1990s, it was a normal taboo that fathers were not raising their families due to the overwhelming issues of drugs, alcohol, and incarceration in that era. My life started the same as most with no biological father in the home. However, I utilized the road God pre-planned to set the stage of how my fatherhood would be in the future. I was raised by my mother, who was the anchor of commitment to family and became the gateway to my introduction to my spiritual father and forever hero called "Jesus."

I remember as a young boy being a little reserved, not knowing what to expect out of life and not having direction, but I remembered hearing a voice saying, "I'm with you." Surprisingly, the voice that I heard as a child surprisingly did not scare me because the sound of my first encounter was so soft and warm. I just felt a sense of safety. Living in a household that was run by four sisters and a strong-willed mother, I had to find my place and my own direction for who I should be. My mother grew up the opposite of me. She had five brothers who all played a vital role in my development, teaching me the principles of being a man and navigating life. Allow me to share with you my journey through the eyes of my uncles. Each experience will demonstrate how their lives and guidance became my driving force going forward.

I will start by setting the scene. My grandparents built a family as an interracial relationship. My grandmother was a fair-skinned woman, while my grandfather was a Black male living in Prince George's County, Maryland. To say their life was tough is an understatement. My grandmother, whom I still consider "the rock," bore five sons and two daughters, my mother being the second to the oldest. As my grandparents' children became older, they had their children. The first four grandchildren all being females was exciting, but for five uncles, I could just imagine their eagerness waiting for the first male to be born. I was the first male grandchild out of now thirty-two grandchildren.

Having no biological father in the home was an instant curse for me, but the part my uncles all played in my life became a profound blessing in the end. My oldest uncle, Tony, set the foundation for who I would become going forward, while my other four uncles set the standard for how I would have to navigate through life. Below are the principles of life and fatherhood I received through their eyes.

Uncle Tony—As a young male, my Uncle Tony represented community. He was once a young Black Panther. My Uncle Tony always stressed the principles of wisdom and how important it is to continue to make the best decisions in life. I remember him always stopping and talking to everyone we encountered in the community. While I am speaking highly of his way of communicating to everyone in the community now, I could not understand why he would stop just to have a conversation which at the time meant nothing to. As I grew older, I realized that what I had to learn from what I was witnessing was the value of patience, connecting with your community, and understanding everyone's worth around you.

Uncle Jeff—Continuing through my journey of learning, my Uncle Jeff would take me out of town as a child to the state of Delaware, where he resided for a short time to be closer to his children. I could remember a time where his relationship with his children's mother came to an end, but it was met with some resistance. I observed my Uncle Jeff having to fight and stand in the face of opposition even when he had nothing to give for the love of his children. As I grew older, I realized what he had taught was that you must sacrifice your own life for the life of others. I grew up understanding that the more you sacrifice of yourself, the more God opens your life up to receive more of His blessings.

Uncle Vincent—This man would be considered as my best friend but overall a teacher of discipline. Every time I was around him, he made everything into a learning lesson. To sum it up, my uncle taught me the value of money and how to always have it for emergencies. I would observe that when people in the family came into hard times, they didn't want to ask him for money because he was so disciplined but knew when it came down to any emergencies, he would be the one to call. As I grew older, I realized what he had taught me was bad days would come, but the people who would survive the struggles of life were the ones who could say yes but had the discipline and strength to say no.

Uncle Eddie—I think the principle I am about to mention is my best trait, and it only came from one man. As a young child, I would observe my Uncle Eddie from afar. Out of the five uncles, he was the hardest to figure out. He spoke with a soft tone, but when he would speak, I was all ears trying to figure out what he would say that would resonate with my future. I learned very quickly from him the value of compassion and humility and that a man can show emotion. Growing up, we were taught that boys don't show emotions, which made it hard to release feelings. My Uncle Eddie gave me the ability to understand that it is okay as a man to display your raw feelings without losing your toughness as a man.

Uncle Teddy—He would call himself the black sheep of the family. The best word I can use to describe my Uncle Teddy is fearless. As a young man, I would observe him the most because we were close in age. My Uncle Teddy taught me to never back down from a challenge and to not buckle in the face of despair. He would do things to me to toughen up my outer shell. I could not stand it when I was younger, but he would always say, "Whatever I do, you will be okay." Sometimes I would wonder what pedigree of man was inside of him to never turn away from a fight. Throughout his life, he gave me a high level of toughness which got me through the military and police academy. He taught me the value of mental strength and resilience. When I went through any tough times and challenging obstacles as I got older, I would hear my Uncle Teddy's voice saying, "You will be okay."

Each encounter with my uncles helped me make decisions in how I raise my children and move through life. I hold close to my heart the experiences I was privileged to witness. I realized growing up that my job was to give back to others unselfishly the same way I was given. I have taught my children how valuable it is to listen to others and take even the smallest thing and store it away, for one day, it will be their time to use it.

Before I close, my grandfather was the center of wisdom in my life, so I have to share two quotes—one he shared with everyone and one he shared with only me. These two quotes brought each principle I was taught by my uncles together for one common good. First, he said, "The wolf that runs the farthest runs alone." As a young man, I didn't understand what that meant. As I got older, it was easier for me to understand. We as people gather as packs like wolves to make change, cause problems, or just worship. I now understand in order to reach your highest level in life after learning all the principles you have, you must first step away from everything you know and lead the pack. The second quote he said was, "Dionta, do you want to be the needle or the thread?" I laughed at him when he asked me because I did not know what he was trying to say. As I embarked on my life, I was able to get the message. There is only one needle. That needle is in the front as the lead. That needle is sharper and harder to break than the thread. The needle pulls the thread and shapes the pattern in which a child, organization, marriage, and community must thrive.

The question from the beginning was, do fathers matter? Without a doubt, yes, fathers matter, and father figures matter the same. The privilege to learn from each of my father figures gave me the ability to utilize each principle they taught me as a tool in life to help navigate through life's many struggles. Someone said to me long ago that any man can be a father, but I don't agree. I believe that only a man who learns the importance of being the needle and taking the lead of the thread will be effective.

Finally, what all of my uncles had in common is that each one of them taught me without knowing. The best way to teach anyone is to lead by example because you don't know who is watching you and learning how to be a man or a father.

A FATHER'S JOURNEY OF LOVE

Altariq Fuller

From an early age, I wanted to be a father. I would dream about being an amazing husband and father to my children. Growing up, not only did my peers seem to not have fathers around, the adult women in life didn't have husbands. I wanted to be different. I wanted to be a husband and a father. I would watch men with their children, thinking, "One day, I'm going to be like that with my children." When I would go places as a child, I would think, "When I grow up, I'm going to bring my children here." When my mother told me "no" to things I wanted to do, I would think, "I'm not going to tell my children 'no.'" As a child, I put a lot into what I would do and what I wouldn't do as a husband and a parent. I grew up without my father being a real presence in my life. I didn't hold a grudge against him for his absence, but I knew I wanted to be a better man. I wanted to be someone my children could look up to, someone they could share their thoughts with, and someone who would be there for them no matter what. I wanted to be a husband a wife could adore. I wanted to take care of a wife and be the head of the household that my family could truly look up to and depend on. I wanted to be what I did not see.

I didn't just want to be a great dad, I wanted to be an awesome husband. For years, I watched my mom parent alone. While I think she did an amazing job, she was not a dad. I wished that she had a husband—someone who would take care of her, show her nice things, and be a good partner for her. For my entire life, I watched her shoulder the burden of raising two Black boys in the hood. My brother and I turned out pretty good, but I'm left to wonder what if my father were present and accounted for? Who would we be? What could we have become if only he was there for us and for her?

My father didn't give me much, but he gave me two beautiful and amazing sisters. We all had different mothers. My father had a total of four children with four baby mommas, and he was not present in any of our lives. This was my orientation to fatherhood, but even as a child, I knew this was not right and that I would do better.

You could imagine my delight when my girlfriend told me she was pregnant with our first son. He was perfect. Ten toes and ten fingers. He was an ideal combination of both of us. Not only was he adorable, he was a good baby. Oh, the dreams I had for us. Our new family. Tina and I had talked about marriage and even started planning, but then came my second baby, just as perfect as the first. He was handsome and strong. I was in love all over again. Before we could get the wedding plans solid, our third child was born. This time, it was a girl. Talk about beautiful. She was gorgeous. Her temperament was great. Wow! And just like that, I was the father of three children. I was in a happy place.

Tina and I struggled, but we were making it. Much of our struggle was trying to get on the same page with our finances. We clearly had different goals for our family. I wanted home ownership to be able to leave something for my children, and well, let's say her priorities were different than mine. The polar opposite goals and dreams for our family brought us to a breakup. This was the last thing I wanted to do, so I tried to make the relationship work. I was miserable. My sister told me, "Just because you are not with their mother, does not mean you can't be a good dad."

My sister was right. I was even more determined to be a good dad. I was able to get my children every other week. I sent them to a private charter school. I stayed in my house where my children had their own rooms and could feel at home and not like guests. We were managing. I loved it the most when it was my week to have them. We would spend time talking, playing, and laughing with one another, sometimes with one another. I felt like despite the breakup with their mother, they were well adjusted children. They were well behaved, smart, and kind children. Just like the day they were born, they were perfect and I was proud to be their dad.

I noticed that my oldest son was different. He would rather play with his little sister than his brother. He would want to play with her dolls and girl toys rather than with the boy toys we purchased for him. I recall shopping with the children, and he would be into the girl fashion way too much. So, why did it come as a shock to me when he announced that he was gay? It shouldn't have, but I guess I was just hoping it was a phase he was going through. Well, not only was it not a phase, but years later, he announced that he is transgender. His announcement caught me off guard. Of all the things I thought my child could come to me and say, this was not on my list.

The day he made his announcement to me, so many thoughts and a range of emotions flooded my mind. "Did I do something wrong? Could I have prevented this? Did someone harm my child? How will he be treated in the world?" You name it, I felt it. By morning, after a night of tossing and turning, I was clear. He was my son, and I would stand by him. I loved this child before he was born, and I still love him. His sexual orientation is not the only thing that defines him. He is compassionate, funny, intelligent, and caring. Most importantly, he is mine.

I researched the internet to get more information about being gay and being transgender. I didn't know anyone I could talk to about this, not because I was ashamed, but because I just felt as if no one would understand. I didn't know anyone who was dealing with this with their children. I became frightened when I read that many youths in this situation have killed themselves due to lack of support and rejection from their family. I definitely did not want that for my child. I made up in my mind before I researched further that I would be supportive and nonjudgmental of my son. I continued my research. I read lots of information I found on the internet and I eventually wound up joining PFLAG. The mission of this grassroots organization is to build on a foundation of loving families united with LGBTQ people and allies who support one another and educate ourselves and our communities to speak up as advocates until all hearts and minds respect, value, and affirm LGBTQ people. There are chapters all over the country, and I was glad there was one near me.

I was nervous going to my first PFLAG meeting, but I knew I needed more information and support. PFLAG was mission critical, because I needed to support and possibly even save my son, not from being gay or transgender, but from low self-esteem or quite possibly even death. I know the world is not kind to people who are different or misunderstood. I knew the world would not be kind to my six-foot, Black, gay son who wanted to live his life as a woman. I needed to get resources to support him through what I am sure was a tough space. He came out while he was in middle school. You know, children can be cruel, and adults would stare and snicker. He was at risk of being bullied, harassed, and discriminated against. I was determined that my home would be a safe haven, a place where he could be himself and be supported and loved unconditionally.

I was sad that I could not provide this level of protection outside of my home. He would have to learn to fend for himself. He would have to learn to be comfortable with who he is. I was determined to make sure he had the support to live his life in a way he could be proud. Well, we went through some tough times, as I suspect all parents of teens do.

What I learned about my son is that he is extremely resilient. He was able to bounce back from all the unimaginable things people said to him and the way people looked at him. He developed this tough exterior and didn't seem to let anyone or anything bother him. He was comfortable with himself, and he began to pursue his dream in the cosmetology industry. I must say, he is amazing. He is beautiful, inside and out. When I reflect on his life, I am so glad that he was born during the time he was. When I was his age, LGBTQ was not widely accepted. While there are still some people who do not accept LGBTQ, there are many more who do. Some organizations support LGBTQ, and thank God for PFLAG, who supported me when I needed it.

A POWERFUL LEGACY

Kevin Greenwood

My name is Kevin Scott Greenwood. I am a married father of two wonderful children living in the Mid-Atlantic Region of the country. I attended Howard University in Washington, DC, where I obtained Bachelor of Science degrees in Physics and Mechanical Engineering. I also attended Johns Hopkins University in Baltimore, MD, where I obtained a Leadership Development Certificate and a Master of Business Administration. I currently work in the Field of Information Technology, and I am also the CEO/Founder of Greenwood Realty, Inc., a real estate firm that specializes in investment and property management. I am also a proud member of The Omega Psi Phi Fraternity, Inc., the greatest fraternity known to man.

I was born to Phebe and Duncan (aka Barry), two beautiful people from Jamaica who came to the United States in hopes of pursuing the American Dream in order to create a better life for their family. My parents were very good to me and poured love and inspiration into my heart from the very beginning. While I love my mother dearly and could talk about her all day, my focus will be on my father. For some strange reason,

West Indians tend to use middle names instead of first names in some cases, which is why my father was called Barry. Everyone called me Scotty growing up, and I didn't know my first name was Kevin until I started going to school.

My father was the strongest man I knew, and he was my idol. He was very popular, outspoken, and extremely intelligent. He received his formal training in nursing in Jamaica and worked as a nurse when he came to America. After a few years, he switched from the nursing field to a supervisory role at the Hersey Water Meter Company. My father worked long hours during the week and was also a disc jockey (DJ) on Friday and Saturday nights to make ends meet. Growing up, there was always music playing in our house, and we always had the latest songs by many different talented artists in the 1970s. I have a great affinity for music and that all stemmed from my father and his huge record collection.

When I was a child, my father owned a brown 1972 Oldsmobile Ninety-Eight Coupe, which was incredible. He even had a portable eight-track tape cassette player that he would slam under his seat when we would hit the streets, and he always had music playing. Of course we listened to reggae, but there was a steady stream of classic 60s and 70s R&B, country music, and instrumental classics, such as *Danny Boy*, played by Sil Austin. I was exposed to so much music at a young age, but the best part of growing up was spending time with my father. He took me everywhere with him, and I always sat in the front seat with no seat belt on, which was a normal occurrence in the 70s. I always remember my father looking over at me with a smile and telling me he loved me. I always felt secure and safe being in his presence, even in adulthood.

My father gave me so many life lessons growing up centered around manhood, honesty, love, and caring for others, so I knew exactly how to behave when he was not around. One day in 1977, when I was approximately seven years old, I learned a very valuable lesson that would stick with me forever. Back in the mid to late 70s, there was a chain of retail stores called Bradlees, which is similar to what a Target store is today. When I was in elementary school, all of my friends would bring Matchbox cars to school, and many wore cool headbands and wristbands. My parents didn't have a lot of money, but we always had what we needed to live comfortably. There was no room for unnecessary items such as headbands and wristbands, but I was always determined to have those extras. During this time, I began to develop a knack for stealing at the stores I frequented with my stepmother and siblings and was always excited to show off what I fenced the evening before. One particular evening, I racked up on a few extra cars and wristbands, and as we headed out to leave, I was intercepted by store security. I always remember going up the stairs to that cold office and seeing a sign that read "Think Fink," which made no sense to me and still doesn't. As soon as this strange gentleman stopped us, I knew I was caught. Once we entered the back room I emptied out all of my pockets and removed all of the items stuffed in my socks as well. Fortunately for me, the security officer let us go, but my stepmother had to tell my father what happened.

My biggest fear was disappointing my father, but getting my tail torn apart was probably an even greater concern. I remember feeling like I was on death row the next day because my father came home after I went to bed that night and left before I woke up to go to school the next morning. I knew the showdown was on its way after school. When my father got home, he had his dinner, and then he came into my room to see me. He lit my ass up harder than I had ever remembered, and then he made me go to sleep. I cried for a while after the ordeal, but I was happy it was over.

The next day when I got home from school my father called from work and asked to speak to me. I wasn't sure what he was going to say, but I remember him saying these exact words. "Son, I am sorry for spanking you last night. I just want you to know that you are always supposed to ask me if you want something, whether I get it for you or not. I have a special love for you, son, so please know you never have to steal because I am here for you."

I was in shock because I knew that I deserved that spanking, but after that call, many things changed for me. I always loved and admired my father, but my love for him grew exponentially, and I knew that his love for me was unique and special. My days of stealing were over, and even if I didn't have the things I wanted, I knew I would be okay without them. As I got older, I was always appreciative of what I had instead of looking for things I didn't really need.

My father was a very good man who worked hard seven days a week and never complained. When he lost his job at Hersey in 1986, I had no idea of the struggles he faced because he would still smile and joke with me as he had always done. I had no idea he was three months behind on the mortgage on our home. My siblings and I were unaware of the money deficit and the worrisome days he had looking for employment at the age of forty-six. He didn't have a college degree, and he never went back to school when he came to the United States to work in the nursing field.

My father reinvented himself by starting a shipping business with a childhood friend who lived in Connecticut. They pooled whatever resources they had together to start a goods and services shipping company called G & F West Indies Shipping, which stood for Greenwood & Ferron. I remember my younger brother and I helping my father load barrels filled with items that customers sent to their family members back home in Jamaica. The West Indian population in Boston is immense, and many come to America to build a better life for themselves, but they always send food, clothing, and many other items back home to their families. My father started out receiving five to ten barrels of items each week and transformed that into shipping countless forty-foot containers of goods during the summer and heavy peak months during the year. He was able to build a multi-million-dollar company within several years of its inception without any formal business training. He persevered and used his intelligence to build the largest West Indian Shipping company in Massachusetts. From his hard work, I learned how a struggle can turn into a great story through perseverance and determination.

Another great attribute that my father exhibited was his love of family and friends. He nurtured those relationships beyond the norm. He always kept in touch with his siblings. I was often awakened on Sunday mornings by his huge bellows of laughter, and I knew he was speaking to one of his siblings about their childhood growing up in Jamaica. My father always opened our home to his closest friends, who often stopped by for food and drinks. Despite the fact that we didn't have a great deal of money, he was always willing to share. I developed those traits with my siblings and friends and often shared what I had with no expectations. I always knew that I would try to share those experiences with my children whenever it was my time to have a family.

My life changed forever on Saturday, August 25, 2007 at 12:02 AM when my daughter was born at Holy Cross Hospital in Silver Spring, Maryland. I was completely overwhelmed with love and happiness when I heard her first cry, and I knew that fatherhood was going to be incredible. Prior to my daughter's birth, I anticipated all of the things I would teach her, the places I would take her, and the time I would spend with her. It was my chance to pass down all of the blessings I received from my father and to enhance what I received for my child. Then my life was changed once again with the birth of my son on Wednesday, December 2nd, 2009 at 12:04 PM.

My father wasn't able to afford to take us on many trips outside of traveling to Toronto, Canada to visit his siblings, so road trips were always a treat for me. I always looked forward to jumping in the Ninety-Eight and listening to music like *Disco Lady* by Johnny Taylor. Seeing my family in Canada was always fun. I had also wished that we could have traveled to other places, such as Disney World in Orlando and other islands outside of Jamaica since I always visited my family there. Now this was my chance to create new traditions, such as trips to Ocean City, Myrtle Beach, Disney World, Turks & Caicos, and many other destinations.

Many have often said that my children are the luckiest kids on earth because I always plan exciting trips for them throughout the year. During the winter months, we go to Great Wolf Lodge in Williamsburg, Virginia and Kalahari Resort in the Poconos Mountains in Pennsylvania. During the summers, we spend time in Ocean City, Maryland; North Myrtle Beach, South Carolina; and Williamsburg, Virginia; to name a few. We regularly go to amusement parks, water parks, and go-cart racing tracks and take outings to Annapolis, Maryland for dinner and ice cream. I simply want my children to enjoy as much of their childhood with me as I did with my father. Now granted, I didn't have the same adventures my children currently have when I was their age, but taking a trip to Grossman's (similar to Home Depot) was just as important to me as a kid. I just enjoyed being with my father wherever he would take me. I thought I was the luckiest kid on earth when I spent the day with my father, whether it was going to look at tools at Sears, fixing a water pipe in the basement, or strengthening a support beam under the rear porch. To me, helping my father on the weekends was the best thing ever!

The time I spent with my father throughout the years always contained teachable moments, whether it was lessons about being a leader instead of a follower, making the best decisions when faced with an immediate crisis, or making sure you look someone in the eye when speaking to them. All of these lessons were taught while we did simple things together, so I do the same with my children at every possible moment. Sometimes when I stare at my children, I remember when I would catch my father looking at me with a smile. Now I truly understand why he would stare and what he had on his mind.

In the summer of 2015, my father was diagnosed with Stage 4 lung cancer, which was a huge surprise to my family because my father visited his doctors on a regular basis. It was common practice for him to go in for multiple checkups during the year, and he would always share the favorable results with me over the phone. I remember when I drove up to

Boston to see him, and as I walked through the door to meet him, he was sitting in his favorite spot on the coach with his arms stretched out toward me. We must have embraced each other with tears for what seemed like hours to me. I remember telling him how much I loved and appreciated all he had done for me; and I even told that story about the spanking for which he apologized, which still pulls at my heart strings to this day. My father and I always expressed our love for each other, and he was never shy about telling me how proud he was about all of the things I had accomplished in my life. I always told him he was my greatest influence and that he was always my hero. For the next six months I visited him regularly and spoke with him almost every day, which was no different from how it always was. We all thought my father would beat cancer, but on Friday, January 8, 2016, his body could no longer house his immense spirit.

In the end, we knew exactly how we felt about each other because we spent our lifetime together expressing it through love, friendship, trust, and life lessons. My father was a person I could always count on. He was one of my biggest supporters, and he was always in my corner. I have already started the same journey with my children, and I am confident that when it is my time to leave this life, my children will be able to express the same feelings for me that I often share about my father.

I love you, Dad.

Scotty

THE RELEVANT "POP POP"

Abdul Jalil

"You are the bows from which your children as living arrows are sent forth."

—**Khalil Gibran,** *The Prophet*

Experience informs this author, and he swears by it that fathers matter, and so did the poet and philosopher Gibran allude to it in his book entitled *The Prophet*, wherein he speaks about children. What follows is a unique case in point the writer shares in an effort to reinforce the noble idea that fathers matter for those men and others keenly interested in the phenomenon known as fatherhood. They are welcome to peruse this author's story to learn what it took for him to personally cherish the role of fatherhood.

Let's begin with who this author happens to be. I am by name Abdul S. Jalil. I am a middle-aged African American man who has been around the block and at the rodeo quite a few times in life. I deem myself fun loving and of fair intelligence. I am always inclined to take "the road less traveled." I am neither an angel nor a saint, but the "ol' man next door" or "that guy who will hold the door for you to enter or exit." I treasure having a good measure and mix of religion and spirituality. All in all, I am just an ordinary guy. Somehow, I made the cut to contribute to this collection; therefore, I have crafted a few cute little words to say a little that might look like a lot. However, it, like me, is genuine. My expectation is that by expressing a couple of ideas, your interest will be piqued to no longer be resistant to the worth of fatherhood. I am, among other things, a husband and the proud father of seven, including one in heaven. It is life loving me, the legend known as "Pop Pop" to five adoring grandchildren plus one on the way. With six sons shining and one daughter glowing, I know all too well what it is like to be joyfully present in my children's lives as well as what it is like to be painfully absent. Employed as a licensed clinician, I provide psychotherapies to countless youth, some of whose fathers are present and others whose fathers are absent. Presence and absence are relative terms, as one could be variably physically present yet emotionally absent, or some meaningful combination of the two. My work with these children, especially adolescents, bears out a phrase that an old buddy of mine used to utter so adamantly that it eventually found a home in my mind. What and how he stated it way back when seemed so simple, but later in life, it became so profound to both my personal and professional ties to fatherhood. What he stated in the midst of whatever we were jibber jabbing about was "father means further." Yes, he gave me a pointer long before its value drew significance to me. In essence, what he was saying all the time was that fathers matter. For all the many years that I knew this old buddy, I never knew of his father, nor did he know much about mine. Ironically, way back when, this old buddy of mine and his blood brothers, all of whom had different fathers, used to tease one another by making disparaging remarks about their fathers as if their fathers did not matter. So, for many years after my earlier trials and tribulations as a father and even more so through work in social services, it clearly surfaced to consciousness that fatherhood has much to do with "further." Furthering the well-being of the children is an essential matter for fathers and no less for mothers as well.

I once heard that somewhere in Africa, when people greet one another, instead of asking "How are you?" they ask "How are the children?" The children's wellness is a reflection upon the relative wellness of the adult (let's assume father in this context). My own wellness eventually came to be synonymous with my kids using such words as "my father," "my dad," or "my pops." Those affectionate references from my offspring came to signify my crowning as their father present-present (here and effective) for them. I have fathered seven children by four wonderful women and have come to the full realization that furthering them was far different then just fathering them, which was major growth indeed.

Historically, the exciting birth, brevity of life, and sad passing of Tamir—my fruit and first-born—along with my then waywardness did not afford me much of an opportunity to forge my way into fatherhood. Tamir passed on from this life at two and a half months from sudden infant death syndrome (SIDS) and ushered on to Jannah or paradise. The birth of Sameerah, my pleasant companion in conversation, transpired while I was away—obviously not present. I was a resident of a youth correctional facility during most of her first three years of Sameerah's life. That experience, compounded with my relative maladjustment at some length after being released from incarceration, rendered me big on fatherhood—my pride and joy—but being variably present and absent was not good for her overall furtherance. The two years that followed the birth of Ibn, my "sun," were a period of relationship woes between his mother and me. These problems and her relocation out of state with Ibn stymied my bona-fide opportunity to be a "present-present" father to him during his primary years of development. The silver lining of fatherhood at that time was that my second- and third-born children were bonded in affection and cast me as their common denominator variably present and absent. For this reason, I wanted my role and image to be positive. The birth and early developmental years of my fourth-born child, Hassan Amir, my handsome prince, joyfully moved the needle in favor of my being present-present in the matter of my parentage. He became the glue that began with clarity to synthesize fathering and furthering. The birth and early developmental years of my fifth-born child, Kamil Ali, my perfect champion, was quite an awakening of being "dad," and it wonderfully became a monumental experience. I became present in all of my children's lives to whatever degree I was able. They were four different innocent, young, and vibrant personalities, and what mattered most was that I was blessed to be the common denominator. A parent plays a critical role in their child's development. If that child's growth has been stunted psychologically and/or emotionally due to some fault of the parent, then it is incumbent upon the parent to participate in the correction of the problem. Donning the crown of parenthood means taking that responsibility. When Wali, my Woo and sixth-born child was delivered at the hospital, I cried near a river just outside of the delivery room. I felt a zing. Providence chose me to be the father of another child—a son. My last three children were born one year after the other, casting a profound effect on my sense of fathering and furthering—of being present-present. My daughter and elder son, although living apart from their siblings, are nonetheless well bonded with them. Living under the same roof with my three youngest children made me believe that my name had been changed to "Hey Dad." Every day and all day, recurrently, it was "Hey Dad" for this, that, or the other. It was often humorous, and at other times, a nuisance. I even once considered purchasing a sweatshirt emblazoned with "Hey Dad!"

Despite all the joy and pain, the sunshine and the rain, my experience with father and further was undercut once again by myself and imposed waywardness—the present/absence variety. That required me to seek help through a thorough recovery process over the span of two years. Once "restored to sanity," I earned a new lease on life and was welcomed into my children's open arms as "dad," once again present. It was nothing less than miraculous, because fathers do matter. The essence of the miracle is that I uncovered my spirituality that had lain dormant through the years. That spiritual awakening made the fact that fathers matter so much more meaningful for me, my children, and the community's children with whom I engaged.

According to Iyanla Vanzant in her powerful book entitled *The Spirit of a Man*, "a flawed diamond still has value." Over time, that value manifested itself in many positive and rewarding ways as witnessed by my children and the children of so many other parents, as it takes a village to raise our children and for them to realize their potential. The matter of fathers being present and participating in that dynamic is so necessary, first in the home, and then in the community. Some years later, with the children all grown adults, I begat still my seventh-born child, Talib, the seeker of knowledge, who is seven as of this writing. I refer to Talib as my bonus. My spiritual awakening has once again allowed my offspring to approach me and say "Hey Dad" with affection. The testament that fathers matter is a continuous confirmation of my resilience and wholesomeness as it is a reflection of that of my kids.

My late blooming blossoms beyond my primary responsibility to my children but it also blossoms through the social and professional facets of my life. Many close friends and associates of my children regard their own fathers affectionately as Pops. Some have even vocalized that they desire redemption for their own fathers who are unfortunately not present-present in their lives for whatever reasons. Within the scope of my work, I show up with the youth assigned to me as a balanced and strong model of a man who matters in their life. Along the way, I plant seeds of encouragement, hope, and a zest to live whole and fulfilling lives. I aim to present as a bow, and with unconditional and positive regard, I view them as "living arrows" in whose lives I play a role in furthering their quest for success. On account of those positive alliances, I draw ardor for my own reinforcement. Gibran went on in his poem to state "let your bending in the Archer's hand be for gladness for even as He loves the arrows that flies, so He loves the bow that is stable."

I vividly recall that although my father was not so strong a bow in being present, he was affectionately my bow. As providence would have it, there were other men in the village, such as uncles, cousins, neighbors, merchants, teachers, and coaches whom I found supplemental in that regard. As I came of age, I realized the void of never knowing my maternal grandfather, as he was deceased. My paternal grandfather was present but not effective in rearing. I have quietly longed to know their stories, the heroics as well their failures.

Fathers matter much in that they have to develop through their own trials and or tribulations and be prepared to leave some meaningful sort of blueprint for successful living to include coping skills, resilience, and problem-solving skills, general guidance, and livelihood options. I truly believe that through my experience, hope, and strength, I have established such a blueprint for all of the children who in some way have been minimally influenced in positive ways by my best example of what it is to be a man, a mentor, a model, and matter-of-fact father. Be blessed. You matter so very much!

SERGEANT

Michael Parker

I grew up as what is called a "military brat" and moved around a lot. My father, James Sr., served in the United States Air Force for over twenty-one years and retired as a Staff Sergeant (Sarg). My dad was my hero and someone who molded me into the man and father that I am today. My dad had three sons (James II, David, and me), and all three of us have daughters. In addition to my father, my brothers and my two best friends played a significant role in my life. I will demonstrate how their roles as fathers assisted me in becoming the dad I am today. My beautiful wife Brenda and I have two daughters— Kaitlyn and Courtney. Kaitlyn is in her second year at Saint Bonaventure University majoring in Communications, and Courtney is freshman at Clark Atlanta University majoring in Business with a minor in Theater.

My mother was present and a factor in my life; however, my mother and father divorced when I was four years old. My mother was a housewife at the time, and she tried to care for me and my brothers as best she could. Without having a job, she realized the feat was too large, and she had to call my father to come get us to stay with him. My dad being a Black man in the military in the sixties was not an easy task, especially being stationed in North Carolina. Not only did he have to battle racism, he had the duty of fathering and raising three boys. My dad introduced fishing to me and my brothers at an early age. This was considered our "bonding time" with our dad. We would go fishing just about every Saturday, weather permitting. No matter how tired he was, he had a commitment to our bonding time.

When we lived in Michigan, we went fishing one night on this old barge and caught a lot of fish. When it was time to go, a family of skunks would not let us leave the barge. The skunks had been camped out at the entrance of the barge, which made it impossible to leave. We ended up staying on the barge until the next morning. We were tired and hungry, and my dad had to go to work that next morning. What a trooper. This is one of so many sacrifices my brothers and I watched my dad convey to us as young boys. My brothers and I watched my father sacrifice so many things to be there for us.

I remember a time we were traveling back home to North Carolina after seeing my grandmother in Roanoke, Virginia and we indicated we were hungry. My father did what any other father would do. He sped up to get us something to eat. While he was speeding, we suddenly heard sirens behind us. The two white police officers told my dad to get out of the car, and my dad wanted to know why. Neither one of the officers responded. They then commenced reading him his rights, placed handcuffs on him, and put my dad in their squad car. The other police officer drove us in our car to the police station. My brothers and I were terrified and did not fully understand at the time what was happening. The police made us sit in the waiting area until our family member came to post my dad's bail. These police officers arrested my dad for going five miles over the speed limit. Wow! As we left the city of Smithfield, North Carolina, my brother pointed to a sign that said, "Welcome to KKK County." That only helped to sum up that situation.

I can remember another fishing story when we lived in Goldsboro, North Carolina. We were fishing by a dam where there were huge catfish and we loved catching big fish. While fishing, suddenly, my father slipped on the rocks and broke his leg. He almost fell in the river; we went running toward my father. He told us to stop, but we kept running because we did not want our father to drown. The three of us plus another man pulled my father to safety. That was close! I could not imagine life without my dad at the age of seven years old.

My dad eventually remarried, and we moved to Roanoke, Virginia. It was my years in Roanoke that inspired my chapter title, "Sergeant." My friends used to call my dad Sarg because he treated our household in a military fashion. Our neighbors used to come to my dad as a male figure for the neighborhood. They would allow him to discipline their kids when no father figure was in the picture. It was determined then that it took a village to raise a family, which I think is still the case in the twenty-first century. Sarg would rally the kids to move a family, pick up bread from the Salvation Army to distribute to the neighbors, or share the fish we caught with our neighbors. When our friends struggled in school or at home, their parents would call him for help.

I remember the last time my father and I went fishing. We had a great time and caught a lot of fish. I often think about him because we fished a lot on the Chesapeake Bay. My dad passed away and went on to glory in 1993 at the age of sixty years old.

I am blessed to have two great brothers; however, sometimes, I wonder about my brothers. For example, there was one incident in Smithfield, North Carolina when my dad stopped for gas and allowed us to use the restrooms. I was the last to use the restroom, and my brothers thought it would be funny to play a joke on me by leaving me at the gas station. When my dad asked them if everyone was in the car, they both said yes. Then my dad realized several miles down the road that one head was missing. They returned to the gas station only to find me there crying. My dad spanked us all, including me, but I dared not ask him why. Even when my brothers and I were not mischievous, we still had to learn lessons the hard way and suffer the consequences of Sergeant's punishments. My dad used his military experience to raise my brothers and me.

In spite of these childhood incidents, I remain remarkably close with my brothers until this day. I was the last brother/son to have a child, so watching my brothers become great fathers is truly reminiscent of my dad. They also worked really hard to provide better lives for their daughters/my nieces.

James began coaching youth basketball in order to teach my niece to play. He even won a city championship with those kids even after going winless in year one. My niece ended up playing basketball in high school and playing intramural basketball in college. My niece holds a degree from Old Dominion University and also referees basketball. My other brother and I used to chant at his games "Coach must go." James discontinued coaching, but he was highly successful in the military and life in general. He was a great father mentor to me and maintains being a great father to his daughter and uncle to my girls.

David (or Tony, as we call him) has also become a great father. He works all the time in various locations, which includes the beautiful Florida Keys. Can you imagine living in the Florida Keys and not fishing? Tony and I have been going fishing together in the Keys for the past fifteen years. We have been fishing all over the East Coast, Bahamas, Cancun, and Jamaica. We promised to keep our fishing bonding time going for as long as we live. Our dad would be proud to know the fishing legacy continues. Tony also allowed his daughter to play basketball and sing in the high school travel choir. My niece holds her Bachelor and a Master degrees from Virginia

Commonwealth University. In between working all the time and going on fishing excursions, Tony also maintains being a great father and uncle to my girls.

My two best friends have also played a huge role in making me a better man and father as I have watched them deal with their kids.

Sam's four daughters have all graduated from college with the youngest going through her internship to become a doctor. Patrick's two sons have been successful as well. One has joined the United States Air Force and the other is pursuing his college degree.

In conclusion, let me tell you about the parenting adventure that Brenda and I share raising two beautiful girls. My wife and I have supported both our children in everything they have done over the years. Kaitlyn and Courtney are both youth members at Galilee Baptist Church. Kaitlyn and Courtney participated in events at Mother's Love Child Care Center, where they were educated when they were young, performing their skills in tap dance, dancing and acting. I also served for six years as the President of the Parent Teacher Conference Aid (PTCA) during their elementary school years. They both participated in choir, band, and PTCA events. Kaitlyn and Courtney decided that they wanted to play basketball, so I became the coach and Brenda was the team mom. As a coach and after coaching, it was realized that I had coached multiple girls and boys who would go on to become Division I athletes.

In Kaitlyn's fifth grade year, an Athletic Amateur Union (AAU) team approached Brenda and me about Kaitlyn's talent, and this began an adventure of travel basketball and our family's yearly vacation. During Kaitlyn's first year playing for AAU, her team went to Orlando for the National Championship tournament. She played well and helped her team to finish in the top eight in the country in her age bracket. Kaitlyn's accomplishments continued to have us spend our family vacations in the gym. She continued to play travel basketball up to her junior year in high school. While watching her play during the AAU seasons at the elite level, it was revealed she had the potential to play at a Division I collegiate program on a scholarship. She played in venues in Tennessee, Kentucky, Virginia, North Carolina, Ohio, New Jersey, New York, Pennsylvania, Georgia, and Florida. Playing in these high-exposure tournaments eventually led to her receiving a Division I scholarship to Saint Bonaventure University.

Courtney's path to success and her journey to college included exploring sports and ultimately challenging her talents in business and theater. While at Skyline Elementary School, Courtney received a proclamation from Prince George's County Maryland for achieving high test scores. Courtney explored her talents in cheerleading, drama, playing the piano and clarinet, singing in the choir, and playing softball. Her drama exposure came about while performing in several summer drama programs. She was casted in four production plays. We realized early on that Courtney was exceptionally talented on stage and that this could be her focused endeavor. She explored softball for the first time in middle school, where she played well, leading her to ultimately play softball in high school in addition to basketball. She continued to blossom at Dr. Henry A. Wise High School, where she carried on demonstrating her talent in the choir and drama. Courtney always had a pulse on excelling academically and used that to her advantage for her college applications. Courtney received numerous scholarships before accepting her offer to attend Clark Atlanta University.

Brenda and I thank God for His grace, mercy, favor, and most of all, His covering over us. We thank God for Tyreese and Anthony McAllister for assisting us with sound guidance and encouragement in the upbringing of our girls. Our daughters are growing up in a social media society and realize these are trying times for their generation. It truly does take a village to raise a child, and we are indebted to our God, family, and friends. Lastly, I would like to thank my Pastor Reverend Dr. Lloyd T. McGriff of Galilee Baptist Church in Shadyside, Maryland for his caring spirit and wisdom and for sharing the vision that God has given him. I am truly blessed and glad that God is a part of my daughters' lives and pray that He continues to be in their hearts and guide their paths. I hope you enjoyed my testimony that I shared with you. It truly has made my life worth living. To God be the Glory! Amen

DISCIPLINE: HANDS-ON, HANDS-OFF APPROACH OF FATHERHOOD

Jerry Todd Reaves

I have witnessed the joys of fatherhood all my life. That feeling of being a father is a blessing from above. I am grateful to still have my father, who is currently in his eighties. To this day, I can recall his teachings, and I continue to pay very close attention to everything he does. I can clearly remember growing up and watching him enjoy being who he is when it comes to fatherhood. He was a silent teacher and somewhat of a laid-back instructor, but his lessons were loud and clear.

When I became a father, the one thing that stood out the most was the way my father chose to discipline me. I'm not even sure if I should use the verb discipline to describe the way he chose to deal with my behavior as a kid. My father didn't do the things I heard others talk about, like being yelled at for not listening, snatched up in the collar until they got the message, or forced to go stand in the corner for hours at a time. Most importantly, my father never chose to physically discipline me.

Over the years, I can recall having conversations with other men in barbershops or while watching sports whose stories of being disciplined as a child were very different than mine. I've been told stories about fathers or guardians who dispensed pain that lasted for days and left memories that have lasted a lifetime—some so severe that the recipients said it felt like ribs were broken. For some of these men, the disciplinary actions came not only in the physical form, but depending on the behavior, could also be emotionally damaging.

One day while speaking with a friend, he happened to share his story of growing up with a father whom he described as a strong disciplinarian. If he failed to conduct himself in a manner that was appropriate to his father, then the repercussions were usually swift and severe. Hearing his numerous stories just blew my mind. He recalled being slapped in the face, punched in the arm, and even kicked in the rear end for doing wrong in the eyes of his father. After listening to all the stories from people with whom I've come in contact over the years, I think I must have grown up on a different planet or was just one lucky kid because I never experienced any of those things from my father. I also learned that their physical discipline came from others, such as uncles, grandfathers, stepfathers, cousins, older siblings or any other family member who felt responsible for their upbringing.

Fathering, I feel, is a learned behavior. It is not something for which you go to school or take certification classes. You do not receive any type of degree, but you do get tested. The test is simple, and the results are not always the end story of how children turn out or what type of parent they become. Fathers raise their children to carry on a tradition of what has been passed down to them. Some of those traditions may be good, and some may be not so good. For me, raising my sons was an easy test, and the only notes I used were the ones I took mentally from my father, whom I consider my favorite instructor of all time.

Now my father, Charlie, has a very laidback and easygoing demeanor—so much so that even as a kid, he never took offense to me referring to him by his first name (I know, a serious taboo in African American culture). As a child, that's the only name I used to get his attention, and I can't ever recall addressing him any other way. It was never dad, pops, or anything like that. He never once corrected me, and never disciplined me in any way for calling him by his name, unlike others who would tell me they knew not to address their fathers by his government name, which most consider disrespectful. I think my father really understood that it was a habit (the question of whether it was bad or good seemed irrelevant to him), and he knew it didn't warrant me being corrected by disciplinary actions. I can remember a particular time when a much older gentleman, even older than my father, looked me in the eye and asked me, "Did you just call your father by his name?" I replied, "Yes, because that's what everyone else calls him." The older gentleman scolded me and said, "If I were your father, I would make you call me dad or discipline you in a way you would never forget." That moment upset and confused me because I never viewed calling Charlie by his first name as being any less endearing, and I have certainly always had the utmost respect for my father.

During a brief separation between my parents, my mom and I relocated to New Jersey. My father, like clockwork, would pick me up on time, driving between Brooklyn and New Jersey, and I would spend weekends and school holidays with him. When I became an adult and then a father, I would reflect back on why he made that commitment to me and to himself. I thought maybe it was because he didn't want to miss out on the everyday teachings of fatherhood. During those trips, I received the teachings of what to do, what not to do, and how to handle the situations that I would most certainly face while transitioning from childhood to manhood. I was taught obedience, self-discipline, responsibility, financial literacy, confidence, and respect for others' feelings and their property. "Do not touch what doesn't belong to you, son" was the strict instruction I received from my father. Remember I told you that my father was a silent, low-key, reserved, and somewhat of a shy type of man? He was. So much so that he didn't give me lessons on the birds and the bees. I never asked either. I would ask questions like "What would happen to someone if they did something terrible and what would be the consequences?" and his answer would be, "They're going straight to jail!" He'd say this laughing, but at the same time putting the fear of going to jail in me. This was an easy lesson, and thank God I listened. I would also ask some crazy questions that at the time I didn't think were crazy. I remember asking one time while we were riding across a bridge into New York, "Hey Charlie, what would happen if a person jumped off this bridge into the water? Would they die, or would somebody rescue that person?" My father didn't answer that question directly. Instead, he took the time to rationalize with me about why a person would even consider doing such a thing of that nature. All those instructions were embedded so deep into my soul that when I became a father, all I had to do was mentally go back and refer to those trips back and forth to Brooklyn. Those weekend trips didn't seem to last very long. My parents decided to reconcile and give their marriage a second chance. I really didn't know what "a second chance" meant at that time, but what I observed and eventually came to learn is that if someone shows themselves to be deserving of a second chance, then give them one.

Fatherhood comes with several requirements, but a major requirement is great patience. Patience is the one thing that grows on you, and you grow with it as well. Having this type of patience gives you wisdom and confidence, which allows you to control your mindset when dealing with children. I felt my father displayed great patience, which allowed him to control his emotions and personal restraint. You see, there was this one time when he almost lost all of the accolades, homage, praise, admiration, and tributes I now give him because one afternoon, I decided I had had enough of what was going on around my father's place of business. Things just didn't seem right to me that day. People were moving in strange ways, and I didn't like what I was witnessing. Now with Charlie nowhere in sight—and I made sure by checking my surroundings because I did not want him to see me handle something I definitely wasn't old enough or capable of handling—I jumped at the opportunity to remove what I felt didn't belong inside of my father's place of business. However, just as I did, Charlie came out of nowhere. He heard every curse word that came out of my mouth that day to get my messages across in my attempt to "clean up" the mechanic shop he owned at the time. Charlie was working on a car, and I assumed he was changing a fan belt on that car because that's what he had in his hand as he swiftly walked toward me. Charlie reached back in a motion as if he was going to evoke harsh discipline upon me with extreme force, but he didn't. Charlie was furious, angry like I had never seen him before in all my eight years. Yeah, that's how old I was using that type of foul language. It was at that point that I saw my father display his personal restraint and great patience. He later explained to me that next time I need to let him handle everything. Charlie's hands-off, hands-on approach instead of physical discipline is the way I was raised and the way I choose to raise my own.

It's My Turn

Fatherhood has been blessed upon me. Now it's my time to shine, my time to display the great lessons bestowed upon me by my mentor, instructor, leader, and friend during my childhood.

When my first son was born, I said to myself, "Okay, Jerry, it's time to show them what you got." When I tell you my fatherhood story is so similar to the one I experienced, it's because I acted accordingly. In a span of less than three and a half years, I had two young sons. Sons will test your patience and willpower, or so I was told. My boys and I would often sit together and play video games. My youngest son was admittedly the biggest sore loser with whom I'd ever come in contact. By the time he was 4 years of age, I recognized his competitiveness as we played racing games. Whenever he realized he was going to lose the race, he would jump up and unplug the game console from the outlet just to say he didn't lose. At first, we would laugh, then laugh some more. Time after time, he would do the same thing, and then it wasn't funny anymore. My oldest son would get so mad, and after a while, he refused to play against him. In their father's frustration and impatience, some children would have probably received a spanking, but my lesson in personal restraint taught me not to overreact in that way. Some years later when they were both in middle school, they were dropped off at home before I got home from work. When I arrived home and opened the front door, the smell of bleach was in the air. These brothers had some type of altercation, and my youngest decided that he needed to spray bleach on his older brother and all of his new school uniforms. Well, I was heated. The kid used the last of my great patience. I felt that this type of behavior deserved physical discipline of some sort. I grabbed the belt, and before I knew it—unlike my father, who had years ago practiced restraint with me—I swung and just nicked him with the buckle of the belt. At that very moment, I realized that I had no clue what I was doing when it came to giving out harsh and extreme lashings. I felt like every physical punishment I evaded, I was about to unleash on my son. I walked away but soon came back to apologize for my actions. Those two had other disagreements following that incident, like all siblings, but I felt corporal punishment wasn't necessary. There was never the need to punch them in the chest, slap them in the face, snatch them up by the collar, or abuse them with such force that it would last for days and leave them with painful memories to last their lifetime. "Come, let me talk to you fellas for a moment" is what I would say to them whenever there was a dispute between them or wrongdoing by them individually. A parent should never raise their children to be afraid of them because I feel that it may destroy their inner child.

I'm not a psychologist or an expert on the rules of discipline, but I do know from life experience that you can get your point across to a child by verbally teaching them how to control their actions. I recently came across an article written by the American Psychological Association, and the content struck me in a very profound way. The article talked about the historical roots of corporal punishment in Black communities. Although so many of us in the African American community share stories that involve belts, switches, extension cords, and the like, the article stated that "whupping" children is not a cultural practice that Africans brought with them to this continent. In fact, the article went on to say that West African societies held children in a much higher regard than slave societies in the Atlantic world, which placed emphasis on Black bodies as property, not as human beings. West Africans believed that children came from the afterlife—that they were gods or reincarnated ancestors who led profoundly spiritual lives and held extraordinary mystical powers that could be harnessed through ritual practice for the good of the community. In fact, it was believed that coercion and hitting a child could scare off their soul. Indigenous people of North America held similar beliefs. As colonization, slavery, and genocidal violence made life harsher for these groups, parenting practices also grew harsher.

This seems so profound to me and only strengthens by beliefs and values about child rearing and discipline. When we take the time to talk to our children, just like my father talked to me, it has a greater lasting impact. I prefer sharing lessons with my sons, such as the importance of thinking before you react and knowing that there are consequences for things you do that can ruin you for the rest of your life. That's the type of discipline I gave my sons instead of throwing punches. They are both adults now, but still to this day, I am constantly instilling in them the knowledge they need to survive in the world today.

FATHERS WHO COVER THEIR CHILDREN IN PRAYER

Stanford Robinson

As a teenager in the 80s running the streets in New Jersey, I was constantly faced with life-changing decisions; but despite all the distractions, I was inspired at an early age to pray for myself because I saw my mother pray. She was a single parent and was a very spiritual woman who prayed all the time. When I was younger, I remember seeing her and I wondered what she was doing because I really did not understand it at the time. As a matter of fact, when my brother and I were young, we used to make the sign of the cross everywhere we went, and it became a habit we picked up as we roamed Jersey. As I got older, I realized what prayer is and I trusted that it worked. We experienced a hurtful loss when our house caught on fire. The fire took everything physical away, but still my mother continued to pray, and her consistency and perseverance to continue to pray through those difficult times taught me a lot about faith-filled trust that God will always be with you no matter what. I was in the ninth grade when I understood the power of prayer. A childhood friend had invited me to go to church with his family. I think that was the experience that truly changed the direction of my life. Attending church with them really helped me understand the value of praying. It was not until I was in the Navy that I started to truly pray for myself and over my circumstances. Something about being isolated at sea so far away from the Jersey lifestyle gave me time to reflect, and I wanted to make it back home.

Once I started praying, I found others that wanted to join in. Crew mates suddenly became prayer partners. Once I became a father, I knew instantly that I would rather suffer than to allow my kids to suffer; so despite my personal trials, I continued to pray over my sons and their lives constantly because there were times in my life where I didn't have anything but God.

I first decided to pray with my sons when we were on the sofa watching a football game. I remember thinking of how I would bring them out to watch me play basketball or them sitting on the sofa alongside me to watch football. I observed how they just watched everything, and that's when I thought to myself, "How would it be if they saw me pray?" I decided then to pray with my sons daily. Now that they are young men, there are times when I don't call them early enough and they will call me and ask me to pray with them. I feel as though it makes my relationship with them as their father stronger. I am setting the tone for how they can maneuver through circumstances. Every time my children are with me, I continually pray with them and over them. When they were young, I established a spiritual foundation that praying does not mean life is going to be consequence free. In fact, from my personal experiences, it was the difficult situations that I had to go through that helped me understand God's greatness, which strengthened my willpower to press on no matter what.

I have a blessed blended family where I am the father to three of my biological sons and to my wife's daughter. I appreciate how different my children are. Sometimes there is one who is a little harder than the others, but you have to stay consistent no matter what and keep on encouraging them. I never forced religion on any of my children. I brought it into our conversations, but it was more important for me to show them how to live rather than to tell them. My oldest son and I forged a solid relationship in his mid-teens. I remember when he was going through a rough patch and he wanted me to pray with him. I told him that I would pray with him and that God would forgive him for his actions, but he still had to deal with consequences. I wanted him to know that even if the results didn't come out the way he wanted, he would still be alright. I have observed far too many times when parents blindly take the side of their children, and that's not the best way to go. That teaches them that no matter what they do, right or wrong, it can be justified. Such blind devotion can ruin a child, ultimately leading to them making poor decisions as an adult. After my son endured his circumstances, we continued to pray. His life changed before my eyes, and my son got on the right track. During his valley moment, I reassured him that as a father, I love him, I'll pray for him, and I want the best for him, but I also made it clear that I didn't agree with what he did because I wanted to be fair with him. Through his situation, my son started to read his Bible, and he told me that he was getting into His Word. I asked my son if there was any time in his life where he thought prayer couldn't work, and he responded, "There is no situation that prayer cannot help." When I wanted to know how he felt when we prayed together, he said, "It means everything to me because you are my Pops. When we started praying together, I was fifteen, and as time went on, you and I began praying every day. Spending that time, you became my friend, and because of our relationship, I've started to pray with my daughter too."

My middle son had a scholarship to play basketball and he worked hard to achieve his dream; but during the process, he had some issues with the head coach. My son became frustrated during the process because he wanted more playing time, and he thought the head coach was blocking his opportunity. As I listened to his valid concerns, he became more eager to leave the program, but I encouraged him to stay. Sometimes it can be difficult to see how much potential your child has just to have an outside barrier creating unnecessary hoops for them to jump through. However, despite my son's determination to leave, I realized that this moment could be a testing ground for his character. He soon came to know that with every blessing comes breakthroughs, which may sometimes feel like breakdowns. I knew that God put a skill inside of him that ranked him to be one of the top players in the country; but I'm not going to lie, it was hard to hear the frustration in my son's voice as he felt like his opportunities were slipping away. I told my son that we were going to pray for game time favor and that the head coach would play him more. A few weeks later, he got his chance. Once that happened, my son just went to work showing off all of skills and passion for the game. Every time, he was called in to play. My son reflects on how things were in his life at that time, and he says "I thought praying wasn't working when I was in college playing basketball, but dad, you kept telling me to keep praying that things would change, which they did! I helped my team win the conference championship, and we went to the second round of the NCAA Tournament." I reassured him that waiting would build his character and get him ready for his next move. My son also told me that "It means a lot to pray together, because it shows me how powerful God is, and it inspires me to want to pray with my kids when I have them." As a parent, you often question the advice you give your children; but as I prayed with my son, I prayed to God as well to lead me and his mom to help him make the right decisions and asked for us to be guided by the will of the Lord and not our own.

My youngest son aspired to play basketball as well, but his interest peaked later in high school, and he was disappointed because he did not receive any offers to attend college. I told him we were going to pray about this and get in the gym and train hard because faith without works is dead. He needed to put in that sweat equity to match his goals. Therefore, in his senior year, he was in the best athletic shape, and as a result of his hard work, he was accepted to a junior college. Shortly after he arrived, they were going to switch to an independent league, and my son told me that it wouldn't be good for his career. I told my son not to give up and that if he wanted to come home, he could. At that point, we didn't know what to do or how to do it, but we prayed and trusted that God would make a way. That was one thing I knew without any question. Moving forward, he came home, he went to a workout, and he showed up and showed out. He was recruited on the spot to a better school where he played and graduated. It was all faith-based, because God showed him favor to come home so he could have the desires of his ambition. My son later told me, "I never thought that prayer was not the answer, because I was taught if things are not changing because of prayer, then I need to change something I am doing." Since I started praying with him, he said, "It has turned into a great habit!"

When I married Reshell, she already had a daughter. I don't believe in saying "stepchild" because when I made a vow to her that I accepted *all* of her, and her daughter is a beautiful representation of my promise. As I prayed with my wife daily and I was praying with my sons, I wanted to pray with my daughter too, because I wanted her to know that she had a praying father. Additionally, my daughter has witnessed her mother and me pray together, and we all pray together and at the end of the day. I want her to be able to see us and one day have a faith-filled relationship with anyone she meets built on solid principles. My daughter is a strong-willed young lady. Her prayer journey is always evolving. As a freshman in college, praying isn't always her go-to solution, as she believes she can figure out a solution on her own. At first, she was standoffish about the idea of us praying, but as a parent, you have to be persistent. As her parents, we often reminded her to pray before she drives, and I would send her daily scriptures. Soon after, we started to have father-daughter prayers, and now when we pray together, she says, "It feels encouraging and it's special." I know that the more you pray with your children, especially when they are young adults, you are instilling a faith of constant covering over their lives and the decisions they make.

As a parent, how do you recognize character-building moments? The only answer I can provide to parents is that before you had a child, you had yourself, and your own personal life experiences will equip you in helping to get your children through their circumstances. I have gone through a lot of struggles, but it made me a better man, and I was able to help my children by using similar situations I went through. My daily prayer is that I don't make it a habit to tell my children what to do but provide them with the knowledge and faith that God will take them where they need to go. I constantly remind them that I'm not always going to be everywhere they are, but God is.

Now that I have established praying as a part of my relationship with my children, I observed a generational gift when I witnessed my oldest son praying with his daughter. I could tell that my son prays with her daily because my granddaughter wasn't just repeating what her dad said—she contributed to the prayer. It was a beautiful experience to see, and my son later told me that he prays with her on a daily basis. Everything that happens in our lives is for our good. I trust and believe that because when my son was going through his valley experience, it caused him to be a better man and father to his child. He went through something that almost broke his spirit; but instead, it built his character. I can understand how important it is to always stay consistent in our children's lives no matter what. Oftentimes, we live our lives in constant adjustment as we grow through challenging circumstances. Although life may have difficult moments, there is always time to make an adjustment.

Sometimes I will call my children, and they will let me know that they already prayed and then they will say that we can still pray again. Those are the moments as a father that make me feel good because my children are taking the initiative in their own spiritual growth. I can see it in their attitude when they say things like "God is definitely great because He's just blessing me with so many opportunities." I constantly remind them that it's not so much what happens to you but how you handle the situation. They have experienced enough life to know that sometimes you want something and pray for that thing to manifest, but sometimes God has something better for you, and you have to trust the process in spite of the outcome no matter what.

My advice to all fathers is that your child should be able to see you consistently praying. Take the time to explain to them what it means to pray. For instance, I have told my children that I cannot be with them twenty-four hours a day, but God can. Overall, being consistent is essential to them. Understand that their mothers are going to pray all the time, but the fathers are the head and the first leaders of their lives. They are watching us to show up for them. Our children see us doing so many things. Why not let them see us pray?

MY LOVE OF FATHERHOOD

J. Rodney Rowland

I am the father of four wonderful Black children. The title of father was mine for the first time in my twenties, fresh out of college and having to learn what that meant. My role of father was extended to include an amazing five-year-old little girl—the daughter of a woman with whom I was in a relationship—and I was more than happy to be that for her regardless of how our DNA matched. As the father of two daughters and two sons, I am fortunate to have the best of both worlds twice over. I am blessed and grateful that my children are by the same woman, because it was important for me to author a new narrative. I always said that I didn't want to have a bunch of children by different women, because as a child, I felt the division it could create, saw the emotion of it all pit adults against one another, and witnessed what could happen if a man spread himself around. I didn't want to do this to my children. From all the firsts to the lasts and everything in between, being here for it all has been my life's joy. It causes me to puff out my chest and smile big. My children are now 19, 21, 28, and 35, and it's been great.

While raising daughters and sons is different, at times even in direct opposition, with all of my children, I am real and I am tough. In the world in which we live, I cannot be passive, especially in the inner city. Growing up in the hood, all parents have to school their children at an early age. Fatherhood is about educating them on the rules of the world around them, including the perils that the streets can hold. Before I had multiple children, I thought not much would change outside of the number, but I've come to understand that just because children are siblings does not mean they will have identical wants and needs. Fatherhood acknowledges that kids are their own people who have their own individuality, and so I handle them according to their personality. I teach my daughters and my sons to go after their greatness, to be responsible, and to enjoy life. Everything I do is with the thought to build a relationship with them that lasts. As they each go through changes and mature, it's nice that they have our foundation to rely on, and I guide them as they go through it.

As a father, I've taught, but I've also learned some valuable lessons as I've raised my children. The main takeaway has been that our fight is not theirs—meaning never confuse bad lovers with bad parents. The love between parents may be lost, and rightfully so, but the willingness to co-parent has to be a step that the father and mother are willing to take for the benefit of their children. Even amid separations, how parents get along matters, and I've learned not to make my fights with their mother fights with our children. As a man, I reached a point where it was not about being right but about the happiness of the kids, keeping the peace, and making an environment full of positivity. Being a good dad has been about being more of the kind of father I envisioned when I was young, more of what I think I missed out on, and more of what I believe a father should represent.

From court appearances to vicious back-biting, cussing each other out down to the ground and ugly fights that spilled over to include family, no matter how their mother and I let it get between us, I did not take it out on my children as some men do. I never cut back time, I never cut back money, and I never cut back on the necessities of living. Unfortunately, some of us think that child support covers or should cover it all. I have had fights with friends about the idea that as long as the money is paid, nothing else has to be done on the father's part. When it comes to your kids, you have to step up and be a man. The children cannot be faulted by parents' shortcomings. Sometimes to have a well-rounded child who will be successful and happy, someone has to be the bigger person because the mental and emotional health of the kids always comes before ego and who did what. I never tried to punish my children or sit by and let them do without. I refuse to withhold that pair of sneakers or a tuition payment because it was not covered by that support order. I don't consider this extra because it's what is necessary and is another way to demonstrate a father's love. They will not forget. My mother taught me this lesson, and I have carried it with me. I refuse to let my contribution be minimized or quantified by anyone other than me or settle for the bare minimum when I know that I am in a position to give my kids all they need and more.

Time matters. I can't say enough how extremely vital this element is to being a good father. Be present. Be active. Be involved. It's key, especially if you are separated. As separated fathers, usually our time is limited, so make the most of it. You don't realize it while you're in it, but time spent with your children can never be reclaimed once they are older and have their own interests. I recommend spending as much time as possible teaching, molding, and exposing them to other things in the world outside of their city so that they get a view of the differences in the world, see other cultures, and use their imagination. Prepare them to leave their comfort zone. Make your mark and leave them with the best parts of you. On so many occasions, all I needed was a tank of gas and a couple dollars in my pocket, and my kids and I were in the car on the open road for adventures to New Jersey, New York, and Maryland. We had the most fun with little to no money outside in the park, playing, running, and exploring. We got to be active, share interests, and connect over stuff from my childhood. Fatherhood is about the money to pay for things and about a man's commitment to investing his time and attention. Spending quality time with my kids over the years, I was able to pour into them, get to know them, and share who I am. Some people say time is short; others say it's long.

Either way, my point is not to waste it when it comes to your children.

There were days, weeks even, when I was steaming mad, when things between their mother and me were at their worst. But once I had my babies with me, all of that was gone. It was time for fun—time to be the daddy. Being a father is an energy, a vibe that made me feel brand new, and I didn't want to bring anything other than that feeling into our interactions. You can save your children from yourself, because as you know better, you do better. Over the years, I have picked the best parts from my parents and from my childhood and used them for myself, but even now, I can see ways that I could have done better. When things have happened in the past, I've wanted to fight fire with fire, but I got past it by realizing that was not the way. We are all human, and when blowups happen, it's only human to want to react. But that's how traditions start, and we continue this same bad behavior and recycle the same kinds of relationships that mirror the unhealthy relationships we saw in our parents. Fatherhood means I set the example because someone has to break the generational curse. I want my children to see my experiences as moments of opportunity to be better than I was and to learn. I never want them to be disgusted by selfish actions that have a long-lasting effect on an entire family when one person does something sneaky and everyone feels it, although they might feel it differently. Your children can act out, have issues in school, and lose sleep because of things you as a man created. Because now their father is gone. Now they need therapy and the extra time and special care to undo the harm. We can pass on trauma if we're not careful. As men, we don't get to talk about what's missing (in many cases our own fathers) or how it affects us and our ability to father. This is not about blame. We are grown men. We know right from wrong. However, we cannot discount environment, influence, and the standard that has been set by our own experiences.

Our children should see us in good relationships. When raising my children, it was difficult at times to maneuver when family and friends interjected their opinions about the type of man I was, and I have friends who've dealt with this as well. Some people do not want to see you with what they do not have and will bring you down. The people closest to us are not always equipped to help and can end up hurting an already complicated situation. At first, this was something on which I harped, and I was preoccupied with the story that was being said about me until I came to see that I was giving too much power to the hate I felt from a woman's loved ones. I decided to shift my focus and look at my own actions and the part that I played in the way I was viewed and treated. I have learned that in order for my children to see love in action, I must put a protective shield around my relationship to keep the union solid.

I'm big on real, honest conversations and transparent communication with my kids about everything that matters, from drugs, gangs, violence, and the police to sexual awareness and self-love. As a father, over the years, I've seen that my kids care about my opinion on what they think, how they interpret what's acceptable, what they deem as destructive, and how they decide who and what to avoid as they grow into adulthood. Listening is even more important. As much as I want them to know what I think, I need to know what they're thinking, how they're feeling, and what's not working in their world so that I not only can help when they ask, but also can try to anticipate or feel out when they need help but won't say anything. My hope has been that by having an open dialogue, they trust me enough with the rough stuff to figure out how to work with their weaknesses when it gets tough. I want them to know that I care by being there to talk about anything, no matter what.

Being a father who loves being a father means checking myself, having that hard conversation when it's just me and my thoughts, and asking how good of a job I'm doing, where I have fallen short, where I can do better, and where I need to step up and supply the demand for a father's love, attention, affection, and direction. My children are my reminder to be my best, because if I'm not careful, if there are too many misunderstandings and mistakes, then my failures could doom their future, and I can't have any part in that. They say a father knows best because we're supposed to use our insight, hindsight, and foresight to guide our children. I have had to be dependable and trustworthy and make sacrifices so my kids can have what I didn't. I have had to help them set their standard for the kind of life they see for themselves and hold them accountable through discipline while offering unconditional love. I have wanted to love them in a way that instills a belief that I am always here to support them, protect them, and call it like it is.

Not only am I proud to be a Black father, but I am proud to be an example of a Black man who loves fatherhood. The role of a father requires responsibility, power, and leadership to keep your kids on the right path, pick them up when they fall, and even push them when they need to fly farther. A father has big shoes to fill. They start by walking with you, and then you give them the strength to walk alone. Being a father is about being a part of something bigger than me that came from me, and will always be a part of me.

I remind fathers everywhere to stay close to their children, and remember, no wasted time, because it goes by so fast. Let your children know that they can do and be whatever they want, and don't just say it. Show it. Make them know it without question. The achievements, joys, and accomplishments of my children are my happy places. Fatherhood is the most rewarding job ever. There is so much significance in a man engaging, nurturing, and helping his children make choices, especially the tough ones. To be a good father, you have to be a good man with good qualities. Anybody I see doing the right thing, I am there to be of service to them so that my children can see goodness in action. Black fathers matter because we're raising kings and queens that are pieces of us out in a world that can be harsh and unkind. They are our circle of life, our bloodline, and our legacy, and I am so thankful.

I had an idea of the kind of father I wanted to be, how important the job was, and how I wanted to show up. Of course, in real life, we do the best we can to live up to our expectations and the picture of how we thought the future would develop. Looking back, I have enjoyed every minute—the teaching moments in all the ups and the downs and the opportunities for personal growth. There is nothing that compares to being a father; and fatherhood is a gift. I will continue to encourage my kids to dream, to shine their light as only they can while they do their best to be great. Despite what some might have the world think, not only do Black men father, but we love it. At fifty-three years old, I would do it again.

FOLLOWING MY ANCESTORS KEEPS ME HUMBLE

Sharif Ali Shafi

My great-great-grandfather, Willis Smith, was very significant in shaping who I am today. He was a bootlegger and sawmill farmer. I am cut from his cloth. More about him later. My maternal grandfather, Big Daddy Bow Willie, had thirty-six children with multiple women. He was a moonshiner and farmer in North Carolina. My paternal grandfather, William Barfield, had twenty-seven children by multiple women. He was a moonshiner. He was a sharecropper during the Jim Crow era in North Carolina.

The Great Migration was the first time I experienced trauma. Both of my parents migrated North from the oppression of Jim Crow, leaving me with my great-great-grandparents. My parents, Ella and Jesse, were part of the freedom fighter movement to fight the system. Around the age of five, I stopped talking for a long time. I believe that my mind and body went into shock during this time that some iconic heroes were being targeted by the FBI. As a little boy, my great-

great grandparents consoled me. I just remember crying for a long time.

This traumatic period also began to shape my character and my belief system. Loyalty and betrayal became huge doorstops in my life. A lot of moving parts were taking place in my life, and the strongest people stepped up in shaping who I am today. My great-great-grandfather and my great-great-grandmother Willis and Mary were born into slavery. Their parents were slaves. My great-great-great-grandmother Viola Anderson was also born into slavery. I met her. Between the ages of seven and ten, I suffered trauma, abuse, and neglect by the Jim Crow South school system. I was bullied for three years nonstop. Neither the students nor the faculty could understand a kid who didn't talk. I began to develop a speech impediment. I was unable to speak in front of people, so they began to test on me, thinking that I was feeble-minded and mentally challenged. Unable to read in front of my classmates, I was placed in a special class. My home life was great. I lived on a very big farm with lots of animals and worked with my great-great-grandfather. He taught me how to hunt, how to make moonshine, and how to protect his wife and property when he wasn't home.

Everybody called my great-great-grandmother Little Mom. She shaped me. She taught me how to cook, how to clean, how to work hard, and how to be honest. She also taught me faith. She also was the family historian. She would tell stories about our ancestors. She was a native American Cherokee Indian. My great-great-grandfather didn't talk very much, and my great-great-grandmother spoke for him quite often. My main chores were to feed all the animals, wash dishes, and help out in the kitchen. They gave me the nickname "Cookie Cake." My other chore was to comb and grease my great-great-grandmother's long, black hair and soak her feet and cut her toenails. During this time, she would share family stories. As a little boy, they didn't mean very much to me. But one story stuck out very much like a sore thumb. She talked about a time when she and my great-great-granddaddy were dating, and they were walking past a car with two white men who said, "Hey you Nigger! What are you doing with that white woman? They called my great-great-grandmother over to the car, and she obeyed according to the Jim Crow laws in the South. She walked over to the vehicle. When they saw that she was a white woman, they flicked a cigar into her chest and burned her breasts.

Looking back, this was a story of honor to my great-great-grandfather. My great-great-grandfather later responded to the cowardly act of violence against his woman. He caught up with one of the men and beat him to death with his bare hands. I can remember asking my great-great-grandfather one day on a hunting trip about the story, and he said, "I'm teaching you how to hunt. You must protect your family with your life." In that moment, my great-great-grandfather became my hero. After that hunting trip, my life changed. I began to speak up for myself at school, asking the teachers for extra work, and I stopped running away from other kids during recess at Sallie Branch Elementary School.

Trauma struck my life again when my stepdad was murdered by three men. One of those three men was a distant relative who robbed him of his money. My stepdad had promised to buy me a red bicycle when he came down from Connecticut. I received my brand-new shiny bike one Saturday morning. My stepdad was a well-dressed businesslike man. He also was a high roller.

That Saturday, we talked about me moving back North with him, but he asked me to stay with my great-great-grandparents and protect them for him. The next morning, people were moving around and very busy. I kept my eyes and ears open trying to understand the conversation. I knew something had happened. It felt like I was losing something again, not knowing that someone had murdered my other hero.

My life took a tragic turn at ten years old. I was locked up at a juvenile reformatory school in Asheville, North Carolina for defending myself. I believe that hurt people hurt people. I stayed in that correction facility for two years. They released me during the gas crisis in the United States between 1971 and 1972.

I can remember leaving my great-great-grandparents' home and returning back to learn that my great-great-grandfather was sick. My great-great-grandfather passed a year later, and about one year after that, Little Mom passed away, leaving me all alone. So my mother came and got me to move back North. It was bittersweet. I really missed my great-great-grandparents more than I missed my mom at that time.

I will never forgive my distant relative for killing my step-dad. Loyalty is everything; betrayal is the worst. At the time I suffered, I didn't understand the significance of these people. They were the shapers of who I am today. My ancestors are survivors of slavery and fighters against Jim Crow. I am nothing without them.

My story has come full circle. I have six sons and one daughter, eight grandchildren, (four boys and four girls), and three stepdaughters. As a Black man, fatherhood is a lot of responsibility and comes with the risk of jealousy, greed, disloyalty, betrayal, lies, and deception. When I became a single father, loving and protecting my children was the easy part. Fighting the Maryland court system to gain custody was the hard part. I refuse to allow another man to raise my sons and daughter. I was taught to be responsible and to protect my family. One of my baby's mothers attempted to charge me with fifty-six years in prison for allegedly abusing my son because she didn't want to pay child support. Fortunately, the judge had a different result to her game plan.

I have one son who was injured during birth, and I sued for malpractice. He was awarded a large lump sum of money. The court system, his mother, and her lawyers took all of his money. These are just two examples of the problems that a Black father must go through when he has seven different baby mothers. Reree was my solid rock from my baby mama drama. She demands nothing, she respects me as a Black man, and she allows me to visit and have my son with no financial strings attached. We raised a beautiful son together in harmony.

Challenging different women in court and winning custody of my children was a daunting task. It cost me a lot of sleep. The job of fathering was not too challenging because I've been directed by my ancestors to raise and protect my children at all costs. I really wanted the relationships with all their mothers to work, but as you can see above, sometimes it is impossible to reconcile these relationships. Playing a metaphorical game of chess with their mothers, using my children as pawns, was reckless. I felt that I had to protect them at all costs. I have also not been able to understand how a woman with whom you live or to whom you are married can abort your child in secret. To me, that is the ultimate betrayal. In order to not injure anyone, we eventually worked out our differences, and I was able to raise my sons under my roof by my rules to become great young men.

I dedicate this to my daughter Nicole, my son Travis, my son Brandon, my son Noland, my son Gabriel, my son Ishmael, and to my children who were aborted without my consent. I want to thank you for allowing me to be your father.

I love you.

Pops

FATHERHOOD: BLESSINGS, BURDENS, BREAKTHROUGHS

Rev. Dr. Harry L. White Jr.

Ethnically, I am an African American. Spiritually, I am a Christian. Vocationally, I am a Baptist pastor. Educationally, I am the product of a historically Black college and university (HBCU) and predominantly white institutions (PWIs). Geographically, since I was born and raised in Baltimore, Maryland, I have a strong East Coast bias. Currently, I reside in Raleigh, North Carolina. Demographically, I grew up in a working-middle-class household. Politically, I am a blend of both progressive and conservative convictions. Generationally, I am a Baby Buster or member of Generation X. As a child of the 70s and 80s, I came of age as African Americans became more visible in media programming. *Soul Train*, *Fat Albert and the Cosby Kids*, *Diff'rent Strokes*, *What's Happening!*, and *A Different World* were among the television shows that influenced my awareness as a child and adolescent. While the aforementioned television shows were influential in my childhood and adolescence, I was always intrigued by the media images of African American fatherhood in the 70s and 80s.

James Evans from *Good Times*, Fred G. Sanford from *Sanford and Son*, George Jefferson from *The Jeffersons* and Heathcliff Huxtable from *The Cosby Show* were some of the African American television fathers who intrigued my adolescent consciousness. While these fictional African American fathers captured my youthful imagination, I felt no compulsion to imagine a different life, as if one of these fictional television fathers were my actual father. My father, Harry White Sr., whom we affectionately call "Pop Pop," is a blend of these fictional television fathers. Pop Pop had the strong work ethic of James Evans, the humor of Fred G. Sanford, the aspirations of George Jefferson, and the ability to encourage like Heathcliff Huxtable. I have also witnessed my father as a loyal friend, a devout church member, a reliable employee, a trusted confidant, a cancer survivor, and a good neighbor.

I have been blessed with a mother and father who have different outlooks on life, yet their personalities complement each other as spouses and parents. While I am my parents' only child, I never felt lonely or isolated because my parents had an open-door policy to family, extended family, nieces, nephews, cousins, and my friends. My parents were intentional about ensuring I could adapt, adjust, be comfortable and code-switch in any environment. My dad was a good high school athlete who imparted his love of sports to me. I grew up around sports in general and in particular on the basketball courts of Baltimore. I cannot recall a time when I was not around basketball. During my childhood and adolescent years, I grew up playing in basketball leagues throughout Baltimore. As a kid who grew up on basketball courts, I showed promise as a basketball player. While I showed promise as a basketball player, my father knew that I needed to be exposed to a different level of competition to take my hoop game to the next level. My dad's desire to see me fulfill my potential in general and as an athlete required his involvement and sacrifice. My dad worked as a milk truck delivery driver for Cloverland Dairy. As a milk truck delivery driver, my father's work hours were approximately 2 am to 12 noon. I have heard my dad describe his job as "bull's work." Delivering milk to grocery stores and convenience stores before dawn is not work for the faint or weak. Having spent his mornings delivering milk to grocery and convenience stores across the Baltimore metroplex, my dad would then take a nap and drive me to the Bentalou Recreation Center forty minutes away so I could fulfill my adolescent hoop dreams. I could have continued to play basketball in leagues closer to our house, but my father wanted to test my mettle by exposing me to a different level of competition.

From ages eleven to sixteen, I played in multiple leagues with teams at the Bentalou Recreation Center in the heart of West Baltimore. I played in Bentalou house leagues, BNBL (Baltimore Neighborhood Basketball League), Project Survival, and the Craig Cromwell Memorial Basketball League and participated in the Bentalou Summer Basketball Camp. This commitment required my dad to drive me to Bentalou at least three days a week. My dad wanted me to excel as an athlete and as a person. As I showed more promise as a basketball player, I got an opportunity to play in an adult spring/summer basketball league. I would compete against grown men in this league. As a teenager, playing with and against grown men will grow your game. The league games were on Saturday and Sunday mornings. This invitation was compelling, but it came with a few challenges. A friend and I launched a lawn care business that required us to cut grass and rake leaves on Friday evenings and Saturdays. On Sunday mornings, church was a priority in the White household. I was a member of the youth usher ministry and youth choir. My parents had no issue with me being involved in activities after church, and at other times, that did not compromise my commitments. However, my parents wanted me to develop a sense of priority and to know the importance of keeping my word.

This life episode occurred over thirty years ago, but I remember my dad asking pointed questions about the lawn care business with my friend and my church commitments. Honestly, I cannot say I was really given an option to play in that particular basketball league. I remember being told the importance of putting God first, commitments, work ethic, priorities, and keeping my word. I did not play in that particular league, but I remember my dad telling me I could play in another league after church on Sunday afternoons.

I took for granted that everyone had involved parents. I really took for granted that everyone was blessed with an involved and invested father. While playing sports, I witnessed my dad become a father figure, counselor, mentor, coach, and transportation service to a lot of my friends and peers. Watching the example of my father formed and shaped my understanding of marriage and fatherhood.

As a young preacher, I was taught the importance of serious academic preparation for Christian ministry. My preparation for ministry led me to attend United Theological Seminary in Dayton, Ohio. During my seminary tenure, I was blessed to reconnect with a college friend, Shauntae Brown. My reconnection with her led to dating, love, and marriage. Shauntae and I were married in May 1998. Having never lived in the same city while dating, Shauntae and I were patient before we attempted to start a family. During the early years of our marriage, Shauntae completed her doctoral degree at the University of Kansas and became a faculty member at Miami University of Ohio. I started a doctoral program at Samford University in Birmingham, Alabama and adjusted to the demands and responsibilities of being a senior pastor.

While we adapted to our new roles and responsibilities, on August 20, 2002, we were blessed with a beautiful baby girl, Nia Imara White. Nia was a precocious, fun-loving child who rarely met a stranger. As a new dad, I felt a greater compulsion to be a priest, provider, and protector to my family. My wife and I are only children. As only children, we wanted to have multiple children. As we tried to conceive our next child, we encountered challenges, but we were blessed with another beautiful baby girl, Kai Simone White, on January 18, 2006. I never envisioned myself as a father to girls, but I am tremendously blessed with the privilege to be Nia and Kai's dad.

My wife and I wanted our daughters to have strong "roots and wings." Thus, we were intentional about exposing the girls to a strong Christian educational foundation. Nia and Kai spent their formative years at the Upper Room Christian Academy for preschool and elementary school. Both girls flourished and excelled academically and socially and were blessed with a strong spiritual foundation. The girls participated in a host of extracurricular activities that included swimming, dance, chess, science, technology camps, golf, track and field, and a host of other activities. As a father, I always saw fatherhood as a calling from Almighty God, and I wanted to be a positive, active, and engaged participant in their lives.

Having been blessed with a good dad, I never wanted my daughters to feel abandoned, forsaken, neglected, or less than valued. If my daughters were involved, then I was going to be involved. I recall the countless fun, enriching moments invested with them on the golf course, spelling bees, dance recitals, swimming lessons, father-daughter dances, field days, bowling lessons, trips to Baltimore and Kansas City, Missouri, and a host of other activities. Fatherhood means being a supportive presence in the lives of your children. Being a father to Nia and Kai has been a tremendous blessing and privilege. As their father, I am blessed to develop friendships with their friends' parents, greater emotional intelligence, and the blessing of reverse mentoring, especially concerning technology, among many other blessings.

Parenting Nia and Kai has been a joy, but the joyous occasions have not come without challenges. As I write this chapter, my family and I are persevering through one of the most difficult seasons of our lives. My oldest daughter, Nia, is healing and recovering from a rare autoimmune disorder. Nia spent over two months in the hospital. Seemingly out of nowhere Nia began displaying behavior that was inconsistent with her personality. Lest we procrastinate, my wife and I took Nia to a local hospital for evaluation. This proactive visit led to the discovery of a medical diagnosis that altered the trajectory of our family's life. Nia, the high school honors graduate, was on her way to Hampton University. Unbeknownst to us, her path to college would be altered because of an unexpected medical crisis. Never in one million years did I envision that my BBG (Big Baby Girl) would be in the pediatric intensive care unit at Duke University Hospital for over thirty days. Nothing prepared me for the anxiety and pain of seeing my child suffer.

During Nia's hospital stay, however, I sensed that God used my father's example to prepare me for this episode in her life. I knew that my encouraging and supportive presence was essential to her healing and recovery. While God and Nia's medical team help her heal from this rare condition, I am relying on God's strength in the midst of my weakness, as well as my father's example, which taught me how to be a father. By God's grace, I am fully confident that Nia will make a complete recovery from this rare disease. I am convinced that God is using my daughter's health crisis as a crucible to prune me. This crucible experience has reinforced some key lessons about fatherhood and challenged me to engage in deep reflection, examine my values, question my assumptions, and discern who and what really matter in life. During this crucible experience, I have reflected on my failures and successes as a man, husband, father, son, friend, pastor, and human being. Since this crucible involves my daughter, I have engaged in prayerful reflection with Almighty God on how I can be the father God wants me to be to my daughters. I am far from an authority on fatherhood, but this experience has challenged me to emerge from this crucible with a greater resolve to be the man and father God wants me to become.

I want to conclude this chapter by sharing some reflections on fatherhood birthed out of my relationship with my father and failures.

> ❯ Believe in your children! Like champion boxers have a cornerman who believes in them, children who fly high in life have at least one person, preferably a par-

ent, who believes in their possibilities. Children need parents who believe in their possibilities. Believing in children endows them with the confidence to aim for the stars and reminds them that the sky is their only limit.

- Have fun with your child! Joking and laughing with your children is an important part of a healthy relationship. Sometimes, children find it impossible to connect with their parents because our dour, killjoy, deathly serious, and morbidly dull dispositions and personalities. They won't forget you are the parent and will know when you "ain't playing."

- Model what you expect! Once upon a time, parents could say, "Do as I say, not as I do." Those days are long gone. There is something wrong when parents expect their children to conform to certain behaviors and habits that they themselves do not maintain. As parents, we need to be authentic models of what we expect from our children.

- Pray for help in raising your children! Parenting is not for the faint of heart, but rather it is a challenging job. No parent is successful in raising children without help from Almighty God. As parents, we need to be constantly bombarding Heaven on our children's behalf and asking God for the help we need to parent for their good and His glory.

⊙ Love your children. Children are a gift from God. As gifts from God, children need to be loved. The words of the song are true: "What the world needs now is love, sweet love. That's the only thing that there is just too little of. What the world needs now is love, sweet love, no not just for some, but for everyone."

Regardless of the inevitable imperfections, faults, failures, and stuff of life, children need to know that their parents love them as precious, unique, and valued gifts from Almighty God.

IMPERFECT MEN: MOVING FROM MANHOOD TO FATHERHOOD THROUGH MENTORSHIP

Rev. Jason Whitley

In this chapter, I want to discuss the importance of male relationships when we move into fatherhood. My prayer is that after reading my story, each reader will be inspired to reflect on the male influencers who shared their views on manhood, on life, and on being a father specifically. I won't use the age-old excuse that I did not have my father around as much as I would have liked. Because the truth is my father's presence or lack of presence did not make me the man I am. My father would not be the only one who would influence me.

I can remember experiences as a young boy growing into manhood in which these men would practically help shape what I have used in the background of my life and the foundation of my belief system. I have had two great-uncles with whom I was very close. One would tell me to drink lots of water and walk slowly. He simply meant don't rush through life and to spend time enjoying it. The other would allow me to have anything I asked for as long as I earned it from him. So, I would cut the grass, do chores for him, and spend my time sitting by him watching his football team on television. I fell in love with the game of football because of him. I have had two pastors who have grown my faith in God. I was a young man when they first taught me the Word. One of the pastors would license me to preach with his blessings at just seventeen. However, this happened a year after he told me that I wasn't ready. He had me sit with my mother and explain why I had the burden to preach. Now, after twenty-five years in ministry, I can truly appreciate why. The other would teach me the heart of what it took to live ministry, including the late-night prayers, phone calls, meetings, and energy spent for the love of God and His people.

I've even had a great mentor who, to this day, challenges me to be the best me I can be and to do and not just talk about what I want to do. He is a significant reason I can be a part of this book. Not only is he a creative author, he has been my friend for thirty years. His influence in my life has helped me to have life-changing experiences. He was a wise advisor and strong force behind my "I can do it" attitude. Yet, as I reflected on what to put into this chapter, my mind went blank, even with all the great experiences of my childhood and my relationship with my father. I put together all the principles and ideas of manhood that made me grow. One of the most important things I recognized and would like to share with you is there is no perfect man. Understanding that concept was vital because it released me from the notion that I must do everything right. That does not mean I cannot try for perfection or excellence. It simply means that my mistakes do not define me and are not an excuse for not being a great father to the three young men and one young lady who call me dad. With my foundation for life being formed and shaped by understanding Biblical knowledge, it is godly wisdom that pushes me to do my best for them. Just like there is no perfect man, there is no perfect father. Your experiences as a man and as a father are not minimal.

So let me go back for a moment and tell you my story as I lived it—my truth as I walk this journey we call life. I grew up with my church and the Washington, DC-area Boys and Girls Club for a big part of my life. If I wasn't at "The Club" in Alexandria, Virginia, I was going to or coming from "The Club." This is where I followed my big brother until I was old enough to join for myself. But from my first day joining to now, this building was more than a building for me. The Club had two of the greatest male counselors the world has ever known. They loved kids and helping boys grow into men. By age thirteen, I was introduced to this man who would alter the way I focus my energy. My mother would say I was rather rambunctious in my youth. He helped me to control the chaos around me. He is the creative author and energy behind this book. He came in as the Program Director for the Urban League in my home town. The program was called the Male Team Responsibility Program, or MTRP. I'm guessing the program aimed to help us make more responsible choices, but I still sometimes make bad choices even now. This program helped me. I can't tell you why it helped or why I connected with the Program Director, but he became my friend and my mentor. Two years later, I would win the Lipton Award for sportsmanship, and just over a year later, the Washington Capital Area Youth of the Year award at seventeen. That was the same year I started using my life to do ministry. That was at the height of my high school football–playing years. My dreams were in front of me, and nothing but me could stop me from achieving them. Just a month before my twentieth birthday, my first son was born. I remember praying over him this simple prayer: "Lord, please don't let me mess him up." The truth is that I instantly loved him and wanted the very best for him. I wanted to give him the best of me and none of my shortcomings. I wanted him to be better than I was and to have the opportunity to grow and follow his dreams. I wanted to protect him from anything that could hold him back from achieving thoughts and dreams. I've had that same prayer at the birth of each one of my children. The thoughts and feelings of love, protection, and guidance never go away.

Fast forward twenty-three years, and what I have learned is that fathers are life-givers. From our physical design and makeup to our responsibility to the people we father, we are designed to stand out and nurture life. Some of the keys to being a good father are love for your child and available access. I have spoken to fathers who often are in their heads about what a good father looks like or what it takes to be a good father in the eyes of that child. Some of those fathers have always been in the home with their children from birth, some have just visitation, and some have had both experiences throughout their fatherhood journey. Nothing negates how that child receives and feels love or the available access to you as the father. I believe that all children think, search, or long for a relationship with their father at some point. It is up to you to create that atmosphere for the children you are responsible for rearing. Within my life as a father, I have been in the home with my children and out of the home from my children, but I don't think I have ever deprived them access to me or my love. Yes, there were times they could not see me as much as they or I wanted, but they always knew in their hearts that their daddy loves them and he wants them.

At the beginning of this chapter, I told you that I would discuss the importance of the male relationships I have had in my life. To do that, I have to reflect on the male relationships that were influential in my life once again. I recognized that I received a level of mentorship from each one of them. Some think of mentorship as only talk and don't take seriously or value the words shared or the wisdom behind them. They will always remain words unless you allow them to inspire and motivate application. What you hear is as important as what you see. Mentorship works under the principles of discipline and accountability. In that regard, it was men who helped to mentor and shape who I still aspire to be. That said, I have not yet become everything I seek to be; it is a lifelong process.

Can't you remember the words of hope and encouragement that came from the men in your life? I am talking about your uncles, cousins, friends, pastors, deacons, and mentors. Men are life-givers. It is the nature of man to give life to things, ideas, and principles in which they believe. These male relationships can help shape your experience as a man and then as a father. These are the relationships you can use to draw your own conclusions. I am not talking about sitting in judgment of them but rather in observation of them. If they have children or wives, watch and learn how they interact and communicate with them, then decide whether or not that works with your belief system. Then challenge your belief system. What is it that you believe, and why do you believe it? How do your beliefs affect the people you love and the ones who love you?

God intended for us to be relational. Consider, then, the age-old Biblical question, "Who is my neighbor?" found in the Book of Luke, Chapter 10:29 (KJV). This Biblical question is based on the understanding of how we relate to people. In the Bible, when Jesus asked this question of the lawyer, he utilized the lawyer's belief system as an influence when approaching his question. We find that when Luke writes of the account, he uses a Gnostic approach. When Gnosticism is analyzed in scripture, it points to an inner belief system in which the writer is reacting. However, Gnosticism in the background of the scriptural text is also used to enlist a reaction from the hearer. Although it is clear that Jesus is dealing with the lawyer's response, Luke is trying to encourage the listeners in his audience as I am trying to encourage you now. So our question is who is thy neighbor? Our goal is to find the importance of connection and learn from the men we are connected to.

Neighbor theology is the common description given to this Biblical text when discussed by theologians. Three textual dynamics exist in this parable. Consider how you fit as you continue to read. The first is that this parable does not identify the person that was left half dead. It does not identify his background, it does not identify his status, it doesn't say whether he was wealthy or poor or whether he was a Jew or Gentile or a Samaritan. The second is that this parable indicates that each passerby is not only void of a level of responsibility, but they each should have had the resources necessary to be able to respond to the needs of the fallen neighbor. Lastly, this parable requires us to consider what we think about when we watch our fellow man's journey. Do we measure the road on which a man has traveled to get to where he is? Would that spark help for your neighbor? We have to understand that the Good Samaritan was not labeled good because of his status but because of his actions, just as a good father is not labeled good just because he is the father but because of how he fathers. Your actions as a father are paramount to fulfilling your purpose as a life-giver.

Sometimes you must step back and examine how you love. Are you a person who believes in touch love? Do you hold onto the blame? Or do you cherish the moments and take time to breathe? Learn who you are and what makes you. I remind myself that love is an action word. Keep your heart available for your children to know you. Remember, there is no perfect man, and likewise, there is no perfect earthly father. We have all made errors in judgment, overreacted, mishandled a diaper, or maybe even missed some time that could have made a moment. Learn what you can from the male relationships you have around you. Learn from those with answers and solutions and not just those with the same problems you have. In some reflections, you might find a better way. In other reflections, you might find another way.

Fathers symbolize hope, protection, and guidance in a world that doesn't take it easy on most. Fathers carry out these tasks by the actions of love. The fact that you are reading this book means that you are inspired to grow as a father. Inside of you is a desire to meet the needs of your children. You need not question your good intentions, but only use them as a platform to become or stay engaged in the well-being and life of your children. This will spark healthy growth in the relationship you seek to have with them. Our children desire our love. As we grow in love every day, let us walk, talk, and live better for them. Fathers are live-givers, so from today on, give life to your relationship with the ones for whom you are responsible. Find someone to whom you can be accountable—someone who is trustworthy and will be honest with you. Allow yourself to be mentored by someone who has your solution.

The truth is, we are all better connected when we are connected to our children and our children are connected to us. Stay available, stay open, and be blessed!

BREAKING THE CYCLE OF ABSENT FATHERS

Michael Williams

I spent close to thirty years working in various roles in the criminal justice system in Washington, DC. In that time, I got to hear the stories of men and women whose lives were adversely impacted by the usual suspects of social ills that we read about in the news every single day, such as poverty, drug and alcohol abuse, and a variety of traumas, including fatherlessness. Many of the people with whom I have worked over the years came from similar neighborhoods to the one in which I grew up and mainly had disengaged fathers or no fathers at all. I always approached my work with the feeling that but for the grace of God, I would be on the opposite side of the desk.

My father was born in 1929 in Washington, DC. He was the oldest of thirteen children. The belief is that my grandfather had a second family living in Philadelphia, Pennsylvania where he had several more children. My father was a man of his time. He worked hard as a baggage handler at the local airport. Most days after work, he went back to his old neighborhood to spend time with his friends at the "clubhouse." He had no clue what it meant to be a husband or father. He went to work, hung out with his friends, and came home and gave my mom the cash he had left after an evening of drinking and gambling at the clubhouse. There was little time spent with my sister and me having dinner, throwing a ball around, or any of the activities that children like to do with their dads.

When I was thirteen years old, my father left our home and moved into an apartment across town. For me, the impact of his moving out did not come until I was much older. Once he left, it became my job to travel across town on the bus weekly to pick up money for my mother. At the time, I did not give it a second thought. I went through the motions and did what my mother told me to do.

In high school, I became a rather good competitive swimmer. I won races and was even featured in the *Washington Post* as Athlete of the Week in the Washington, DC, Metropolitan Area. This was a big deal for my family, including my father, who had something to brag about even though he had not attended a single swim meet. One of my most vivid memories of that time was the DC Public Schools Swim Championship. I remember right before starting my most important race looking up into the bleachers and seeing my father walking in. I was so excited to have him there and was determined to show him what I could do. Sadly, after winning the race, I looked up to where he had been sitting and saw an empty seat. Later that week on my trip to pick up my mother's money, he said to me, "You almost won that race," even though I did win that race and every event in which I participated.

By this point in my life, I was accustomed to him not being around much. I was a senior in high school and was preparing to head off to college to continue swimming. My coach at H.D. Woodson Senior High School was an incredible father figure for me and the hundreds of kids who came through the program. Coach was and still is a man of God who set an example of a Godly father. I could not have articulated it at the time, but his presence gave me a vivid picture of what a father should look like. Coach had five children of his own, but he always made time for the kids on his team. He was more than a coach. He was a father figure. He was tough on us kids, but he was also patient and encouraging. I recall getting into a fight with one of my teammates. He was so angry with both of us, but when he got me alone, he expressed how disappointed he was in my behavior and told me that I was better than that. I did not know what he meant at the time, but I thought long and hard about what that meant. Looking back, I'm sure he had a similar conversation with my teammate, but at the time, he made me feel as though I was special and that I had more in me than getting into a petty squabble with a teammate. He taught us many valuable lessons, such as never quit. Even when you feel like giving up and that you will not win, quitting is not an option. He taught this in the context of swimming, but it was a life lesson that I have carried with me throughout my adult life. This lesson has served me well in the context of marriage, parenting, and my career.

It took me a long time to realize the impact that Coach had on my life. It was not until I was an adult with children of my own that I realized that I needed to figure out what type of father I wanted to be. Once I became a father, I thought about what I needed to do for my sons to grow up to be good men. I realized that my presence was number one. I needed to be there to help them to navigate the many challenges that they would face as African American boys and men and to allow them to chart a course to become successful and productive men who could build on a family legacy that in large part would start with me.

I married my college sweetheart shortly after graduation, and we started our family almost immediately. Becoming a father was the most incredible event in my life. My oldest son was born on Christmas Day in 1995, and my youngest son came eighteen months later. I was terrified of becoming a father, but I was determined to be fully committed to the endeavor and provide my sons with the type of dad that I always wanted while growing up. I made sure that I stayed active and engaged in their lives from the very beginning.

My wife and I agreed that raising these boys to be "good" men was our primary objective. We tried to instill in them a commitment to excellence along with a sense of responsibility to themselves, their family, and their community. I watched these lessons take root during my mother's final years. She lived with us for the last several years of her life. Toward the end of her time, she was weak and frail. Of course, it was my responsibility to care for her, but I watched in amazement how my sons stepped up to help care for their beloved Nana. They would check on her to make sure she had everything she needed. My oldest son even wrote about his experience taking care of his grandmother for his college essay. This was a significant moment of pride for my wife and me, as it seemed that the lessons we had been trying to teach were manifesting.

As I think about my journey as a father, I recognize that I did not always get it right. When my boys were young, I worked several jobs to make ends meet. When my oldest son realized that my wife and I had names other than Mom and Dad, he made a connection that had a significant impact on me as a father. While we were talking one day, he stated that mom's name was Tiffany and dad's name was "work." I recalled being floored and realizing that I had to make a change. I did not want to be one of those fathers who focused primarily on providing material things to his family, but still, I wanted to have a positive impact on the lives that they would eventually lead. I ultimately gave up the part-time jobs and turned my focus to my full-time job as a parole officer and to raising my sons. I did my best to attend every parent-teacher conference, school play, and sporting event in which they were involved in. While these events were sometimes exhausting, they were also great opportunities to show up for my boys and connect with teachers, coaches, and others who were a part of their lives.

When my sons were young, we started regularly attending church. At the church we joined, I saw men committed to their children in ways that I rarely saw in person but saw on television. While I wanted to be that type of father, I did not know how. I participated in several small groups with men who seemingly were grappling with similar issues. One of these small groups was called Men Leading the Charge. Of all the essential lessons learned in that group, the one that stuck with me the most was that at some point, every man needs to decide who he is going to be, and if that man experienced a childhood with an absent father, he had to actively work to break the cycle of absent or disengaged fatherhood. He had to be the one to change things for his immediate family and future generations.

According to the most recent U.S. Census, more than 1 in 4 children live without a father in the home. As a criminal justice professional, I saw the results of these absent fathers every day. The men and women with whom I worked in the justice system suffered from many social ills. Many of them grew up in poverty, struggled in school both academically and socially, and of course found themselves involved in the criminal justice system with all the associated problems that it causes. When talking with these men and women, I often heard stories of how they wished they had a father or father figure in their lives to teach them how to avoid the many dangerous behaviors in which they were engaged. One of my primary motivations for working so hard to raise my boys was that I never wanted to see them end up in the justice system.

My sons are now in their twenties and have both graduated college and started their journeys. When I reflect on fathering them when they were younger, I realize that incorporating God into our family was key to their development. We made sure to pray each day before leaving for school and work. We attended church regularly and stayed involved in various ministry activities. I think this gave them a sense of purpose for their lives. They both care deeply about others and are preparing for careers and lives that have a positive impact on others. For several years, each Easter, my wife and I took the boys to a local shelter to serve meals to the homeless. I recall both of my boys being enthusiastic about serving the men at the shelter and its impact on their world view.

As I mentioned previously, I was very intentional about attending every event in which they were involved. At times, this wasn't easy with all my other responsibilities. However, I never saw it as a burden. I enjoyed every school play, concert, and sporting event. I loved watching their talents grow and blossom. I encouraged them to try different things. The only requirement we set was that once they started a task, they could not quit. Others were depending on them, and they had to be responsible and meet their obligations.

During their teen years, my focus was on getting them prepared to go to college and start their careers. In hindsight, I could have done more to build our relationships. As men, we often focus on the developmental aspects of raising our children. As my sons have entered adulthood, I would like them to see me as a resource for unfamiliar situations in which they find themselves and not feel like they have to figure things out on their own. I am now realizing that even though they are young adults, my role as their dad continues, and I thank God for that every day.

DADDY ISSUES

Ron L. "Kashaun" Williams

Introduction

Daddy issues? Do you have any idea how difficult it is for a man to consider, much less acknowledge, that he just might have "daddy issues"? Isn't this a notion reserved for women who, as adults, still find themselves seeking the affirmation that they did not receive from their fathers? Indeed, it could not apply to men, especially those who grew up all dude. Could it? This is a question that those of us who grew up without fathers in our lives must confront. Did not having a role model in the home affect our parenting, relationships with our kids, our decisions, our marriages, or the people we choose to befriend. If so, how?

Too many of today's Black fathers grew up like me—without a father in the home. Nevertheless, there's no escaping the inevitable. We grow up, fall in love, and before we know it, get married and find ourselves in a delivery room. Of course, that's the conventional route. No need to entertain alternatives because no matter the means of transportation, we have arrived at the same fatherhood table—the very same table as those who had the benefit of both parents, all praying for the wisdom to produce healthy, happy, and productive children.

Early on, I thought that if I could do most of the things that my father didn't do, it would be enough. I didn't realize that I was being fueled by proving to him, my mom, the world, and myself that I was a good man and a better father than he could ever have been. I wanted to be able to say, "I made it without you."

Your little bundle of joy arrives, and you realize that it doesn't come with an owner's manual. Where were the classes for this daddy thing? Not only is there no manual, there's no "return to sender" label either. I dove in determined. I had no idea that I would discover years later the impact of not having a role model had on my decisions and actions. I had to come to grips with this and the notion that I just might have "daddy issues."

My Story

This notion didn't just occur to me out of the blue nor did the solutions arrive gift-wrapped on my doorstep. It arrived after years of reflecting on moments and events that had occurred in my life. The most notable occurred while attending the funeral of a colleague and fraternity brother's father. Initially sadness, my feelings turned to ones of envy and outright jealousy. More about that later. First, allow me to share my upbringing.

I was born in New Smyrna Beach, Florida, and I grew up in Newark, New Jersey. At the time of my birth, my father was twenty-three and my mother was eighteen. By the time I was two, my parents had separated, and my mother and I moved in with my maternal grandparents.

In 1962, my mother decided to move to Newark in hopes of establishing work that would afford her the ability to take care of me. The move made little sense to me because I thought that she had a great job. She was in charge of all the clothes at the store where she worked and would bring home tons of them. It wasn't until I reached adulthood that I learned that she was not permitted to try clothes on in the store.

In 1963, when I was seven, my mother attempted to move me in with her. However, it wasn't until 1966 that Mom found the means to support us both. In the interim, I remained with my grandparents, seeing my father occasionally and often in a drunken stupor. Still, I looked at him as my dad, even after discovering that two boys I had known as long as I could re-member were my half-brothers. It was at the home of a female classmate who happened to be the cousin of my yet-to-be-discovered older brother, Claude. She lived two houses from my grandparents, and her father was a drinking buddy of my father. One of her older sisters took pleasure in irritating me, and this day was no different. She seized the opportunity to tease my brother and me about having the same father knowing we had no idea. Both in disbelief, our tempers quickly rose. The next day, I shared the events with another cousin who not only confirmed that Claude was my brother, but she also informed me about my younger brother, Tony. At the time, Claude was in the fifth grade. I was in the fourth grade. We were in the same class, as the grades were combined. We literally faced each other every day.

By the time that I was fourteen, my father had sobered up, remarried, and given his life to Christ. Nevertheless, our relationship was all but non-existent. He offered no support to my mother, and yet I continue to visit him, albeit out of obligation. We had little to talk about, and he seemed as anxious as I for the visits to be over.

What little of a relationship we had dissolved upon the passing of my grandmother. I was a 21-year-old college junior and had come to attend her funeral. As it was my custom, I dropped by for a visit, but he had not gotten home from work. I departed on foot for my aunt's house and on the way ran into a cousin who shared that my father would be passing through to drop off his carpooler. Within minutes, he came driving by. I guess I was expecting some expression of empathy. Instead, he slowed down, peered at me, and drove off. The subsequent ten-year period of neither seeing nor speaking to him is an indication of how I felt. That period ended when my ex-wife insisted on messing up an awful relationship. She wanted to meet him and for him to meet his granddaughter.

Until his death in 1992, I continued to visit my father when I was in town. However, I never made a trip for the sole purpose of visiting him, nor did he ever visit me. His sudden death caught me by surprise. I guess in the back of my mind, I had hoped things would end up differently. Whatever feelings I had were suppressed or channeled into my children.

In later years, I realized how much his absence had influenced how I parented and the decisions that I made. The feelings that I thought didn't exist had been surfacing in other forms and areas of my life all along. If I wanted to exorcise these demons, I had to acknowledge their existence and cope with the reality that I had daddy issues.

Things I Learned Along the Way

Face Your Demons

I had to face my demons, or better yet, my reality. My Uncle D would say, "Boy, just because you can out talk and think quicker than most, I don't buy your own BS." That was his way of saying, "Don't lie to yourself." His words helped me realize that I had been in denial. I had been suppressing my feelings, and in so doing, I had allowed my dad to influence my decisions and actions. Undoubtedly, he had also influenced me as a husband.

My children were seven and three years of age when my father passed. I was bitter, and I felt that his death robbed me of ever having the closure that I had wanted and the chance to show him how good of a man I had become. I wanted him to acknowledge me. Subconsciously, I was seeking approval. I suppressed a lot in those days. That's how I coped with things that I thought were out of my control—suppress it, suck it up, and move on. Isn't that the mandate and mantra for Black men?

At the urging of my pastor's wife, I agreed to write him a letter. She suggested that I pour all of my anger, bitterness, and any other emotion into it. It worked because I can't recall a thing it said. What I know is that I stopped feeling bitter and resentful.

Another bit of unanticipated help came from a reliable and expected source—my mother. A mother just knows, as they say. I called to check on her, but somewhere along the way, the conversation shifted. For some reason, she felt the need to remind me that my father was never my responsibility, but instead, I was his. Any failure was in him failing to be my father, not in me failing to be his son. She said that my father was her choice. She then charged me with fulfilling my obligation to my children. I needed those words.

Love Your Children More than You Fear Failing Them

There are no perfect parents. Surprise! You are going to make mistakes. Accepting that can be liberating. When my daughter (the oldest) arrived, I quickly discovered what unconditional love meant. The birth of my son only deepened this understanding. In many ways, his arrival represented a chance at redemption. While my daughter was and still is my baby girl, my son's birth was my chance to show that I could be a good father to a boy who looked just like me. In many ways, I saw myself in him.

During their teen and young adult years, I learned that I had to love them enough to provide the tough love and discipline that they needed as individuals. In the beginning, I was so concerned with maintaining a good relationship that I compromised decisions. I am confident that they would disagree. I prayed for the courage and wisdom to make the right decisions. While my children could have passed for twins, they were their own unique individuals. I had to invest the time to understand what moved them as I made decisions. Most importantly, they needed to be able to see through my words and deeds that they were loved by their father. They are now both over thirty, and my daughter has three children of her own. The methods will change, but parenting never stops. Know that love won't let you fail them.

Give Them What You Have

Parents want to give their children a better life than they had. We want to see our children grow into the fullness of their potential. I didn't want my children to do without the things that they wanted and indeed not the things that they needed.

In my quest to give them all that I didn't have growing up, I fell short of giving them the things that I did.

Each of us has gifts and talents, and we all have our crosses to bear. Teach them what you learned from overcoming your trials. Teach them to appreciate hard work and sacrifice and share your experiences. Like Grandma's recipes, pass them on. Most importantly, allow them to face adversity and work themselves out of problems into which they have gotten themselves. Don't be too quick to bail them out of their messes.

Give Them A Reason to Cry

I said it. Give them a reason to cry! I don't mean screaming, "If you don't stop crying, I am going to come in there and give you a reason to."

Earlier, I mentioned that while attending a funeral, my feelings of sadness suddenly changed to envy and jealousy. I attended the funeral and all subsequent events, including the repast and family gathering after that. After hearing guests go on and on about the great relationship my friend had with his dad, I was left feeling confused. This went on all day. My friend had three older siblings, but you wouldn't know it. Even in their speeches were references about my friend's relationship with his father. The stories and memories were special and were a testimony to what it meant to have a father in their life. I became resentful.

Several weeks later, my friend and I were having lunch, and he shifted into a conversation about how much he missed his dad. Before I could catch myself, I found myself going in on him. I told him how fortunate he was and how much I envied him. He had memories, and he knew without a doubt that his father loved him. I had no such memories.

My father had passed two or three years earlier. As I entered the church for his funeral, a woman offered tissues, which I declined to accept. I remember thinking, "Why is she offering me tissues?" It wasn't until I arrived at my seat that I realized she was offering them to the family. I nearly got offended when I realized that this woman thought that I was actually going to cry over this man. The only feelings that I could muster up were those of resentment and bitterness. For me, there were no fond memories. There were no private or special moments, no inside jokes, no times that he came running to the rescue. There was no looking out into an audience or stands to see a proud, smiling father at any event in my life.

To hear how strong a relationship my friend had with his father made me realize that I wanted the same with my children. Since then, my mission has been to build that kind of relationship and to provide my children with enough laughs, special moments, and memories that they, too, will have reasons to rejoice and cry at my homegoing.

It's Your Cup

Finally, there is no magic formula. If there was, I would have had it copyrighted and marketed by now. We each have to face our truth by examining all aspects concerning our personal situations. Things look different from the front than they do from the back. To change or better understand what you see, sometimes you only have to change your vantage point. Invest the time to examine your life and the effect that not having a father may have had on you. Master the skills that you have. Your children are different, so establish individual relationships.

How you choose to view things will be critically important. It's not whether or not your cup looks half empty or half full that distinguishes whether or not you are an optimist or a pessimist. That will depend upon whether your goal is to fill or empty the cup. The truth is it is a half-cup, and the true beauty is that it's your cup. You can empty it and fill it with something else. As I said, there is no magic formula. These are your children—your gifts from above. Your mission is to fill their cup until it runs over. Give them all that you have.

I align and join my prayers with you on your journey to be the best father that you can be. Give them a reason to cry.

Daddy issues? Not me, not you, not anymore!

About the Authors

Anthony J. McAllister is a husband, father, and Q-Pop to his only grandson, Zyir. He is a dedicated father and husband and has been happily married to his lovely and incredibly supportive wife Tyreese for the past twenty-eight years. Anthony is a leader in Alexandria, Virginia and Prince George's County Maryland and has served the City of Alexandria for the past twenty-eight years as a Juvenile Probation/Parole Officer. He is an ordained Deacon and a proud thirty-three-year member of Omega Psi Phi Fraternity, Inc. Anthony was appointed to the Prince George's County, Maryland Commission for Fathers, Men, and Boys, and he and his wife are the owners of Clinical and Forensic Associates, a private mental health practice and consulting firm located in Upper Marlboro, MD. He and his wife are co-founders of The Ayana J. McAllister Legacy Foundation.

Learn more at www.anthonymcallister.com

John Bannister, PhD, is a father, photographer, educator, and advocate of innovative ways to approach sharing knowledge has committed himself to developing learning experiences through his work as a professor, trainer, and creative. Holding degrees in business and education, Dr. Bannister also owns and operates JBPhotography, a photography business in which he captures people, places, and things. He recently published the book *America Through My Eyes* (https://store.bookbaby.com/book/america-through-my-eyes), which curates a photography project in which Dr. Bannister spent at least one night in each of the fifty states (and the District of Columbia). In this work, he highlights one image from each of the locations visited and his insights on this four-year journey.

Dr. Bannister can be contacted via email at johnbannister1974@gmail.com or john@jbphotography2016.com. You can also connect to him via Instagram or Facebook @jbphotography2016.

Emmett Burke is an entrepreneur, an educator, a father, and the CEO of Ascending Counseling Solutions, Lewis & Burke Real Estate Company, and Lewis & Burke Insurance Agency, and the founder of The Entrepreneur Leadership Foundation non-profit organization. He attended North Carolina Central University. Emmett graduated cum laude with a BS in Political Science. He is a former Richmond Public Schools and Chesterfield County Public Schools teacher. Emmett is committed to eradicating chronic miseducation and generational poverty on a local and global level by inspiring and motivating children, teenagers, and adults to become educational and business leaders in their community. He is family oriented and devotes his time to his wife and newborn daughter.

Rev. Dr. Robert F. Cheeks Jr. is distinguished as a gifted teacher, an anointed preacher, and the Senior Pastor of the Shiloh Baptist Church of Odricks Corner, Virginia. Dr. Cheeks leads Shiloh with a Christ-centered passion for life-transformation and social justice. In addition to serving the local church, Dr. Cheeks also serves as the Co-Chair of the Fairfax County Criminal Justice Reform Team with Virginians Organized for Interfaith Community Engagement (V.O.I.C.E.). Dr. Cheeks earned a Bachelor of Science degree from Morgan State University, a Master of Divinity degree from the Howard University School of Divinity (where he was the recipient of the Henry B. Maynard Exegetical Preparation and Preaching Proficiency Award), and a Doctorate of Ministry degree from the United Theological Seminary. Dr. Cheeks resides in Maryland with his beautiful wife, Min. Constance, and their amazing son, Nicolas Micah.

Learn more at www.robcheeks.com

George E. Coker was born and raised in the inner City of Philadelphia, PA. He is the oldest of seven. He enrolled at Shaw University in the fall of 1986 on a basketball scholarship and majored in Business. In November of 1990, he was charged with the murder of a friend and was and sentenced to life in prison. While in prison, he was determined to finish his college education and earned his Bachelor of Science Degree in Business Administration/Business Management from Shaw University's Cape Program in 2008. During his thirty years of incarceration, Mr. Coker has engaged in extensive self-help so that he can better himself to become a productive member of society. Upon his release, his plans are to obtain his master's degree in Sociology to serve his community and help as many people as he can. His four beautiful grandchildren serve as motivation for him to be the best grandparent and mentor that he can be to other men who are striving to have a relationship with their children while incarcerated.

Dionta L. Douglas was born on January 29, 1978, at Prince George's County Hospital in Cheverly, Maryland. In 1992, Dionta enrolled in Eleanor Roosevelt High School in Greenbelt, Maryland. In 1994, he attended Old Dominion Vocational School in Lynchburg, Virginia, receiving a GED/Certificate from Home Builders Institute Plumbing Trade. In 1996-2009, Dionta joined the United States Air Force as a F-16 Fighter Jet Aircraft Inspector. Dionta excelled in the Air Force, being recognized for achieving the highest level of an Aircraft Inspector. In 2008, Dionta met his current wife, Radeesha Brown, while raising 5 children. In 2009, he joined the Maryland State Police as a State Trooper. He founded a youth program honoring the legacy of fallen hero Wesley Brown in March 2013. Dionta currently has twenty-four years of service while continuing to teach youth in Prince George's County, Maryland's criminal justice system and supervise upcoming State Troopers.

Altariq Fuller is a son, brother, and father. While many men claim these roles, Altariq embodies each role. As the eldest son, he demonstrated his unconditional love for his mother when he became her sole caretaker after a stroke limited her ability to care for herself. He is the only brother to his siblings, and standing over six feet tall, he was always the protector. His role as father was the role in which he took the most pride. For a time, he was the custodial parent and relished in the idea that he was a single dad and was solely responsible for protecting and providing for his children. Despite not having his father or a male figure after whom to model, he wanted to be the best at each of his roles. If you were to ask his mother, siblings and children, they would agree that he is the best.

Kevin Greenwood currently works as an IT Project Management Consultant for General Dynamics. Kevin is also the Founder/CEO of Greenwood Realty LLC, specializing in Investment and Property Management. Kevin holds BS degrees in Physics and Mechanical Engineering from Howard University and an MBA from Johns Hopkins University.

For several years, Kevin has Chaired Gamma Pi Chapter's Social Action Program, which is one of the most important mandated programs in the fraternity. Kevin has been an active Board Member of the Ayana J. McAllister Legacy Foundation since 2017. He has also served as an Assistant Coach of several Upper Marlboro Mustang teams, including the 9U Maryland Buccaneers team for the Fall 2019 Season.

While Kevin continues to serve in the Prince George's community, his most important role is being a dedicated husband to his wife and father to their two beautiful children.

Learn more at www.IAMKEVINGREENWOOD.com

Abdul Jalil is originally from Newark, New Jersey and currently resides in Linden, New Jersey. He is the prized husband of his gifted wife, Trina, over the past eight delightful years and gracefully moving forward. Providence chose him to be the legendary father of seven children and five grandchildren, plus one other on her way. He is a graduate of Rutgers University in New Brunswick, New Jersey, with a master's degree in social work and is licensed in New Jersey as an LCADC and social worker. He is presently a therapist and has served adults and youth in the fields of HIV/AIDS, addiction, and health insurance.

To connect, email him at abdul_jalil700@yahoo.com

Michael Parker is the husband to the lovely Brenda F. Parker and father of two beautiful daughters, Kaitlyn and Courtney.

He holds a bachelor's degree in Information System Computer Security from Strayer University and is currently employed with the Department of the Air Force, serving as an Information System Security Manager on the largest acquisition program for the past seventeen years. He was raised in a military household and joined the military after high school. He served seven years in the United States Army and was deployed to duty in the Operation Desert Storm. He is a Deacon at Galilee Baptist Church in Suitland, Maryland and a dedicated community servant.

In his leisure time, he enjoys fishing and had the pleasure of coaching both of his girls' basketball teams.

Jerry Todd Reaves is the blessed father of two adult sons, the youngest of five children and the first in his family to graduate from college. Jerry is a proud alumnus of Shaw University (1990), one of the nation's oldest historically Black universities. He currently serves as Vice President of the North Jersey Alumni Chapter. A native son of Brooklyn, New York, Jerry is an avid sports enthusiast who is fanatical about the Baltimore Ravens, Boston Celtics, and New York Yankees. Over the years, he has coached and mentored dozens of children. He is also the Founder of Prom Time Sponsorship, a youth organization dedicated to financially sponsoring prom attire for underprivileged graduating seniors. When he's not serving the City of Newark as a Project Coordinator, you can usually find him listening to house music, traveling, or relaxing with a good cigar.

Stanford Robinson is a Christian man who covers his family through the spirit of discernment and his everlasting faith. His hometown of Newark, New Jersey is where he shares childhood memories with his identical twin brother and younger sister. After growing up in Newark, he decided to explore the world and enrolled in the United States Navy for ten years before being honorably discharged. He now lives in Maryland. He is married to his beloved wife of four years, Reshell Robinson. They have successfully merged their blended family and are proud parents of three sons, a daughter, and a magnificent granddaughter.

Stanford Robinson has established lifelong roots in the DMV area as both an active member and Deacon at Galilee Baptist Church, located in Suitland, Maryland. He also serves his community as a church instructor for "Raising Kingdom Kids," which is a course offered at Galilee's Growth Institute.

J. Rodney Rowland is a father of four, a hard worker, and a Philadelphia native, who graduated from Shaw University. He began his career in the Philadelphia School District teaching middle and high school for five years, and later pursued a career in real estate and construction in the Philadelphia area, where he has worked diligently for the last twenty-two years. Rodney joined the Laborers Local Union of Philadelphia, where he has been Chairperson and Auditor for two years. He has spearheaded an annual Black Friday Coat Drive for the last seven years for shelters throughout Philadelphia. He's a dedicated member of Christian Compassion. In Rodney's spare time, he loves cooking and spending as much time as he can with his family and children. One day, he'd love to open his own soul food restaurant and cross it off his bucket list.

Sharif Ali Shafi has thirty years of experience in mental health and law enforcement. He is a graduate of West Virginia State College, a member of Phi Beta Sigma fraternity, and the proud father of six boys, three girls, and eight grandchildren (four boys and four girls). Sharif is the CEO of multiple companies in which he teaches youth to be dominant in sports and advocates for those who cannot speak for themselves. He also coached in the NFL for five years. He curates a global exhibit called "The Lost Man Shaming of America," shining a light on injustice, police brutality, and reparations for the African descendants of the slaves in America. Sharif's great-great-grandparents, Willis and Mary Smith, are two of his greatest inspirations and taught him the important lesson of always protecting himself.

Learn more at shaficares.com

Rev. Dr. Harry L. White Jr. is a visionary Christian leader who has dedicated his life to advancing God's Kingdom. Reverend White was born and raised in Baltimore, Maryland. He is an honors graduate of Howard University, Washington, DC, where he received a Bachelor of Arts in Journalism and African American Studies. Reverend White holds a Master of Divinity from United Theological Seminary in Dayton, Ohio and a Doctor of Ministry from Beeson Divinity School in Birmingham, Alabama.

Reverend White is a proud member of Omega Psi Phi Fraternity, Inc. He is also a best-selling author of several books. In 2019, he was inducted into the Martin Luther King Jr. Board of Preachers at Morehouse College. Reverend White has served as pastor of Watts Chapel Missionary Baptist in Raleigh, North Carolina since June 2006.

Reverend White is married to Dr. Shauntae Brown White. They are the proud parents of Nia and Kai.

Rev. Jason Whitley is a native of Alexandria, Virginia. He received and accepted his calling to ministry early in life. He was ordained on December 10, 2017, by the Ebenezer Baptist Church in Alexandria, Virginia.

Rev. Whitley attended college at Virginia Union University and Liberty University. He is currently pursuing his Master of Divinity degree while enrolled in graduate studies at the Samuel Dewitt Procter School of Theology at Virginia Union University in Richmond, Virginia.

Rev. Jason Whitley has served in ministry for twenty-five years. He has been a willing servant to his community. Rev. Whitley has served as Director of Evangelism, Assistant Youth Pastor, Children & Adult School Bible Teacher and as Superintendent of the Sunday School Ministry throughout his service to the church. Lastly, Rev. Whitley loves God, sharing the "good news," and his family.

Learn more at www.revjlwhitleyministries.org

Michael Williams is the father of two amazing sons and has been married for twenty-seven years. He attended Lincoln University in Pennsylvania and American University in Washington, DC where he earned a master's degree in Public Administration.

Upon graduation from college, Michael began his criminal justice career in the District of Columbia, working for both the city and federal governments. Following his retirement from government service, he transitioned to the Pew Charitable Trusts, where he leads justice reform initiatives throughout the United States.

Michael is an active member of the First Baptist Church of Glenarden where he serves in ministries that focus on men and married couples. He also serves as a Commissioner on the Commission for Fathers, Men, and Boys in Prince George's County, Maryland.

Michael has committed his personal and professional pursuits to the service of others.

To connect, email him at mikeowms@verizon.net

Ron L. "Kashaun" Williams, while new to the writing scene, has spent a lifetime in the coaching, mentoring, and leadership game. If you asked him what he did for a living, he would probably smile and tell you, "I practice applying the Word of God in my life daily." Then he would laugh and say, "Oh, you meant what do I do for money?"

Ron grew up in Newark, New Jersey as the only child of a single mother. In this book, he openly shares his personal story of how he came to grips with the effects of having an absentee father. If you are also the product of a single mother or know someone who is, his chapter, "Daddy Issues," is for you.

Ron graduated from Clark Atlanta University and is a member of Omega Psi Phi Fraternity.

To connect, email him at kashaun875@yahoo.com

SPONSORS

The Ayana J. McAllister Foundation is a non-profit organization whose mission is to deliberately engage communities of color disproportionately impacted by gun violence through advocacy and education strategies. In March of 2017, co-founders Anthony J. and Tyreese R. McAllister founded the 501(c)(3) after their 18-year-old daughter, Ayana, was killed by gun violence while she and her sister, N'Daja were home from college on spring break. The McAllisters, having lived a life of public service and ministry, quickly went into action, triumphing over the tragedy. The foundation's intention is to contribute to the significant reduction of homicide, suicide, and acts of violence that result from irresponsible use of firearms in Black and Brown communities.

www.ayanamcallister.com

Clinical & Forensic Associates is a private counseling and consulting firm. Our professional therapists work with individuals, couples, and/or families facing one or many of life challenges, including but not limited to depression, anxiety, trauma history, or current crisis. We strive to improve the emotional well-being of clients by providing collaborative and client-focused therapeutic services that align with the belief that the client is the expert in their own life but desires to identify and address current and long-standing difficulties in experiencing more joy, and alleviating suffering and self-defeating thoughts and behaviors.

www.clinicalforensicassociates.com

CREATING DISTINCTIVE BOOKS
WITH INTENTIONAL RESULTS

We're a collaborative group of creative masterminds
with a mission to produce high-quality books to position
you for monumental success in the marketplace.

Our professional team of writers, editors, designers,
and marketing strategists work closely together to ensure
that every detail of your book is a clear representation
of the message in your writing.

Want to know more?
Write to us at info@publishyourgift.com
or call (888) 949-6228

Discover great books, exclusive offers, and more at
www.PublishYourGift.com

Connect with us on social media

@publishyourgift